THE CHAMPIONSHIPS
WIMBLEDON
Official Annual 2000

JOHN PARSONS

Photographs by
CLIVE BRUNSKILL, GARY M. PRIOR and STU FORSTER
of Allsport Photographic

Publisher
RICHARD POULTER

Editor
JOHN PARSONS

Production Manager
STEVEN PALMER

Publishing Development Manager
SIMON SANDERSON

Art Editor
STEVE SMALL

Managing Editor
ROBERT YARHAM

Publicity and promotion
ANNALISA ZANELLA

Photography
CLIVE BRUNSKILL
GARY M. PRIOR
STU FORSTER

Photo Research, Allsport
ELAINE LOBO
KER ROBERTSON

Photographs copyright © 2000 Allsport Photographic

This first edition published in 2000 by Hazleton Publishing Ltd,
3 Richmond Hill, Richmond, Surrey TW10 6RE

ISBN: 1-903135-00-1

Printed in England by Bath Press Ltd

Colour reproduction by Barrett Berkeley Ltd, London

Results tables are reproduced by courtesy of
The All England Lawn Tennis Club

This book is produced with the assistance of Canon

FOREWORD

The Millennium Wimbledon Championships were a great success by any measure.

Pete Sampras claimed an extraordinary seventh title by defeating Pat Rafter amid emotional scenes in the men's final as darkness was descending. He thereby won his thirteenth Grand Slam singles title, eclipsing the previous record he shared with Roy Emerson.

Venus Williams triumphed in the ladies' singles to win her first Grand Slam singles title — surely there will be more? She beat in turn Martina Hingis, the top-ranked player in the world and number one seed; then the reigning US Open Champion, her sister Serena, and in the final she overcame Lindsay Davenport, the defending Wimbledon Champion.

In the doubles events there were more emotional scenes as the 'Woodies', playing together here for the last time, won their sixth title; while the Williams sisters came back on the third Monday to win the ladies' doubles in front of a packed Centre Court crowd, who together raised over £28,000 for the 'Kids on Court' charity via their reduced price admission.

During the fortnight there were several really memorable matches. Pat Rafter's five-set win over Andre Agassi offered tremendous rallies and great excitement, as did Venus Williams's quarter final triumph over Martina Hingis, where the contrast in styles gave us all a wonderful contest — the irresistible force versus the immovable object.

To celebrate the Millennium, we held a parade of former champions on Centre Court on the middle Saturday. In all, 64 champions were presented to HRH the Duchess of Gloucester, the Honorary President of the LTA, to the delight of a huge television audience and the Centre Court crowd. Special cheers were raised for Rod Laver, two-times winner of the Grand Slam, happily recovered from a stroke last year, and Bjorn Borg, five-times winner of the men's singles, who was returning for the first time since his last memorable final with John McEnroe in 1981.

Wimbledon 2000 also saw the opening of our new Millennium Building with fine new facilities for the players, the press, umpires and Club Members/LTA Councillors. These enhancements proved very popular.

The Championships continue to attract worldwide attention. They were televised in 180 countries and our web site received a record 2.34 billion hits.

I very much hope you will enjoy this record of Wimbledon 2000 which gave so much fun to so many people.

Tim Phillips
Chairman of The All England Lawn Tennis & Croquet Club
and the Committee of Management of The Championships

INTRODUCTION

ONCE again, as Wimbledon approached the general consensus among players — and bookmakers — was that Pete Sampras remained the player to beat. On the eve of Wimbledon 2000, the 28-year-old American remained the outstanding favourite, although this time that was due, at least in part, to the lack of concrete evidence otherwise.

The number of players capable of winning the world's most prestigious tournament was no less than in the past. One could list at least six, and probably as many as eight, capable of success, including two former winners, Andre Agassi and Richard Krajicek — the latter being the only player who had beaten Sampras at The Championships in his last 47 matches.

Yet on the evidence of the first half of the year, one could produce an uncomfortable list of reasons why all of them, including Sampras, might not win after all and that there was a clear opportunity for a new champion to emerge.

The most obvious candidate in this category, many felt, could be the Australian action-man, Lleyton Hewitt. As he had demonstrated in winning the Stella Artois Championship at Queen's Club eight days earlier, he has everything it takes to win a major title on grass — a fine serve, blistering returns on both flanks and the ability to move swiftly and confidently on the surface.

Some talked in terms of a possible quarter final between Hewitt and Sampras being the key to the fortnight. What Hewitt still lacked, however, was the experience of playing in the later stages of a Grand Slam. There was a further problem. He had been drawn in the first round against the handsome American, Jan-Michael Gambill, equally well equipped on grass, who had nothing to lose and had made it clear he was going to relish the chance to create the first major upset of The Championships on Centre Court.

While support for Sampras was unwavering, his lack of matches following injuries earlier in the year, meant it was not expressed with quite the same conviction as in the past. At the same time everyone knew that the moment he walked through the gates of the All England Club, whatever worries there were over his form and fitness would pale alongside that cloak of invincibility which would do its best to inspire him once more as he sought that record-breaking 13th Grand Slam title in the event which would simply add to his delight.

There had been times during the first six months of the year when Sampras's star had not shone so brightly as one had come to expect. The same could be said, however, of the previous year's runner-up, Andre Agassi, who, on the evidence of his tennis at the French Open and Queen's Club, had certainly lost some of the intensity which had made him the Australian Open champion in January.

Naturally everyone in Britain was hoping that Tim Henman, after reaching the semi-finals and then losing to Sampras in the two previous years, would again be a major contender, especially as this time he was in the opposite half of the draw to the champion. One theory was that the recent poor results registered by Henman and Greg Rusedski might be a help rather than a hindrance inasmuch that they would lessen expectations and thereby the pressure.

Henman, though, was in by far the toughest section of the draw with the prospect, if he reached at least the fourth round, of then having to beat Mark Philippoussis, Agassi and the rapidly revitalised Pat Rafter in successive rounds just to reach the final.

While Sampras would clearly have preferred to have played more tournaments in the first half of the year, that was even more so the case with Lindsay Davenport, the defending ladies' singles champion. Injuries had restricted her to only four matches since the end of March and deep down one sensed that even she was setting out on another seven-match journey more in hope that total belief.

For much the same reason there was very little pre-tournament spotlight on the Williams sisters, Venus and Serena, both of whom were clearly potential champions. Most forecasters seemed to overlook how close Venus, in particular, had been to making it into the final in the two previous years and concentrated instead on the need for Martina Hingis to start adding to her list of Grand Slam titles once more, after failing to do so in the last five of them.

Hingis, naturally enough, wanted to make amends for the way her emotional problems on and off the court 12 months earlier had contributed to her losing in the first round to 15-year-old Australian, Jelena Dokic. On her day Hingis has the talent and, thankfully, in these days of growing power, still the touch and style to win. On the other hand there had been a growing number of occasions in the previous year when she had been made to look vulnerable against such big-hitting heavy hitters as Davenport, who she was projected to meet in the final — and the Williams sisters.

IT'S PLAYED FOR THIS, B

UT IT'S WON WITH THIS

POTENTIAL.
IT'S THERE TO
BE REALISED

Canon is proud to be an Official Supplier to The Championships, Wimbledon.
http://www.canon-europa.com

pete SAMPRAS

andre AGASSI

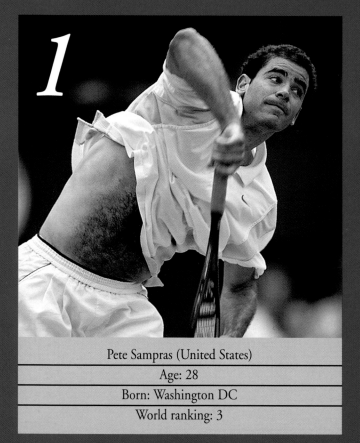

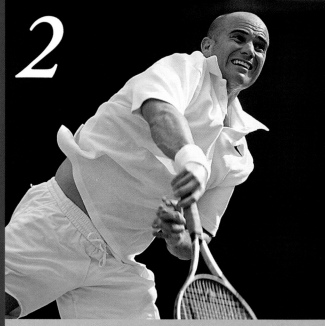

Pete Sampras (United States)
Age: 28
Born: Washington DC
World ranking: 3

Andre Agassi (United States)
Age: 30
Born: Las Vegas, Nevada
World ranking: 1

By universal consent, Pete Sampras was again the man to beat. And no wonder. When he retained the title in 1999, becoming Wimbledon champion for the sixth time in seven years, the American equalled Roy Emerson's record of 12 Grand Slam men's singles titles.

12 months on, despite being limited in his matchplay by injuries in the early part of the year, he was the overwhelming favourite not only to establish that record as his own but to equal Bjorn Borg's achievement as the only man to win at least one Grand Slam title in eight consecutive years.

Sampras's many skills, principally his wonderful ability to vary an array of winning serves, his attacking forehands and those spectacular 'slam dunks', have seldom been more effectively demonstrated than on the immaculate lawns of the All England Club.

At the same time Sampras, who announced his engagement to American Bridgette Wilson in the week before The Championships, was well aware of how every year the task gets tougher.

Some of the impetus in the resurgence of form and confidence Andre Agassi had demonstrated in the previous two years may have been lost in recent months but he still arrived at Wimbledon leading the entry system listing, the equivalent of the old ranking list, which reflects year-round performances.

The swashbuckling Agassi has all the adventurous flair one would expect from someone who was brought up and still lives in the flamboyant city of Las Vegas. And, as he has shown by becoming the first man since Rod Laver in 1969 to win all four Grand Slam singles titles, that adds greatly to his natural abilities as a player.

Agassi won Wimbledon way back in 1992. Should he triumph again, he would join Jimmy Connors as the only player to win his second singles crown eight years after his first.

From the age of four when he was filmed hitting with Bjorn Borg and Ilie Nastase, interest in the life of the charismatic American, on and off the court, has always been paramount and needless to say has not diminished since his romance with seven-times ladies' champion, Steffi Graf, was revealed.

magnus NORMAN

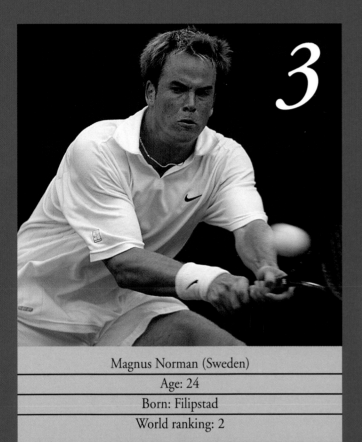

3

Magnus Norman (Sweden)
Age: 24
Born: Filipstad
World ranking: 2

gustavo KUERTEN

4

Gustavo Kuerten (Brazil)
Age: 23
Born: Florianopolis
World ranking: 4

One of the first memories most Wimbledon fans will have of Magnus Norman was when he was forced to default from the fourth round in 1997, after he had overcome a heart murmur problem, and survived 46 aces in upsetting Goran Ivanisevic in the previous round.

Later that year, to make sure his career could continue, he underwent a five-hour operation to correct the congenital irregular heartbeat, since when he has hardly looked back.

The statistics tell their own story, from 52 in the rankings going into 1999, he is now firmly established in the top echelon and his progress was fully reflected in the way he reached the final of this year's French Open.

Norman's ability to play well on all surfaces, with his heavy-hitting forehand often the key, is well sustained by all the training which has enabled him to develop the enormous stamina evident in his five-sets victory over Andrea Gaudenzi in the opening rubber of the 1988 Davis Cup final in Milan.

Although all of the eight titles Gustavo Kuerten had so far won on the international circuit had been on clay, most notably his second triumph at the French Open two weeks earlier, there was also plenty of evidence to support his increased confidence on faster surfaces.

Last year, seeded at The Championships for the first time, he justified his 11th placing by reaching the last eight before losing to Agassi, while on hard courts he went on to reach the same stage of the US Open and this year he pushed Pete Sampras to four sets, three of them tie-breaks, in the final of The Ericsson at Key Biscayne.

Kuerten would be the last to suggest that he is a potential champion at Wimbledon, at least not yet, but he has the right mixture of power and subtlety in his game, as well as a resilient determination, which can cause plenty of problems for others along the way.

He is also one of those players, increasingly rare these days, who almost always looks as if he is enjoying himself on court — a mood which is happily shared by spectators.

yevgeny
KAFELNIKOV

cedric
PIOLINE

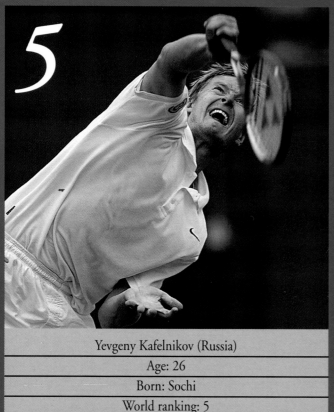

Yevgeny Kafelnikov (Russia)
Age: 26
Born: Sochi
World ranking: 5

Cedric Pioline (France)
Age: 31
Born: Neuilly/Seine
World ranking: 6

Yevgeny Kafelnikov is one of those players who many feel could and probably should have achieved more at the highest level than one French Open title in 1996 and one Australian Open crown last year.

At his best, the man who last year briefly enjoyed a spell on top of the world rankings, produced the quality of tennis which few could resist on any surface. On other occasions, his head drops, the unforced errors flow faster than winners and his record inevitably suffers.

So far on six visits to Wimbledon, Kafelnikov, who is never afraid to say what he thinks and is only too aware of his own mental frailty at times, has only once gone beyond the third round.

Indeed he is better known for losing a two-sets lead against Tim Henman in a first round match in 1996, two weeks after triumphing at Roland Garros, than anything else which has happened to him here since. Never disregard him, though, for he certainly has the ability to be a major contender if fit — and in the right mood.

It is ten years since this amiable Frenchman first played at Wimbledon, with his greatest moment coming in 1997 when he became the first Frenchman since Yvon Petra in 1946 (the last champion to wear white flannels) to reach the final.

He lost to Pete Sampras but he had beaten former champion, Michael Stich, and Britain's Greg Rusedski along the way, to demonstrate the strength of his game on grass.

At first glance Pioline does not appear to be unduly athletic but once on the move, he can be one of the quickest players about the court. His best strengths are his serve and returns, two of the most vital qualities for success on grass.

Those characteristics were also the key as he beat Tim Henman on a medium-pace indoor court in the Rotterdam final in March, the first of the two titles he has won so far this year. Mentally strong under pressure, he won the most tie-breaks (30) on the ATP Tour in 1999.

lleyton HEWITT

tim HENMAN

Lleyton Hewitt (Australia)
Age: 19
Born: Adelaide
World ranking: 7

Tim Henman (Great Britain)
Age: 25
Born: Oxford
World ranking: 14

Even before he lost to him in the final of the Stella Artois Championships at Queen's Club this summer, Pete Sampras described the exciting Australian teenager as 'the future of tennis'.

Few who have seen this feisty, all-action, always-aggressive teenager surge through the first half of the year, winning four titles in the process, would argue with that. Although lightweight in physique, Hewitt is already recognised as a heavyweight in terms of talent and above all commitment.

An outstanding junior, who would probably have followed his father, Glynn, into Aussie Rules Football had he been taller and bulkier, that game's loss is undoubtedly tennis's gain. In addition to an increasingly effective serve and a brilliant capacity to return on his forehand and his double-handed backhand, Hewitt also moves exceptionally well on grass.

The fearless Hewitt arrived at Wimbledon having recorded at least one victory over all those ranked above him, bursting with confidence, and with many convinced that, if not this year, it may not be too long before he also succeeds Sampras in even more illustrious circumstances.

After Tim Henman became the first British player in Open tennis history to reach the semi-finals for a second successive year in 1999, the belief that he might well become the first home champion since Fred Perry in 1936 inevitably gained momentum.

Some disappointing performances on his way into The Championships, when he failed to survive a round at either Queen's Club or Nottingham, at least dampened down some of the expectations — and therefore, one hoped, some of the domestic pressure he was bound to be carrying — though not Henman's own desire and determination.

He went into his seventh Wimbledon convinced that, although his results were not so impressive as 12 months earlier, his game was constantly improving and maturing.

As always the key would be how well he served, hit his still sometimes unpredictable forehand and above all maintained his concentration at the level which only Pete Sampras had defied on the Centre Court in the two previous years.

martina HINGIS

lindsay DAVENPORT

Martina Hingis (Switzerland)
Age: 19
Born: Kosice, Slovakia
World ranking: 1

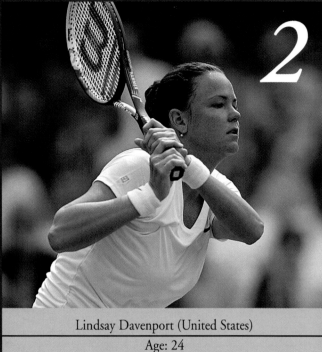

Lindsay Davenport (United States)
Age: 24
Born: Palos Verdes, California
World ranking: 2

The summer of 1999 was not the happiest of times for Martina Hingis. Emotionally distraught after losing to Steffi Graf in the final of Roland Garros, her mother decided not to stay with her at Wimbledon, where the Swiss teenager was beaten in the first round by the even younger Australian Jelena Dokic.

Hingis's determination to put those bitter memories behind her this time had never been in doubt... and although back on top of the world rankings, she had not entirely wiped the slate clean with her super-critical French fans by losing in Paris to Mary Pierce in the semi-finals.

Wimbledon, therefore, where she won the title in 1997 as a 16-year-old then became an even bigger target especially as coming into this year's tournament she had not won any of the four Grand Slam titles for more than a year.

An astute all-round player, with a wide range of elegant, as well as well controlled strokes, Hingis had been working to improve her strength and her already impressive speed about the court, to help her combat that extra power which lies in the hands of Lindsay Davenport and Venus Williams in particular. She was certainly the favourite.

Asked if she could successfully repeat the superlative grass court form which made her the champion a year earlier, Lindsay Davenport said 'It's a tall order. It will only be possible if I manage to discover that magic form which carried me through a year ago.'

On her day there is little doubt that the 6ft 2in American, who makes full use of her height and reach, can produce the most irresistible tennis on the immaculate Wimbledon courts. Her powerful serve is the key, for it is usually the shot which, if not bringing her an immediate easy point, helps her open up the court for a winner to follow.

Yet Davenport's instinctively aggressive, sometimes risky, game leaves little margin for error, which was why she was concerned about her lack of matchplay coming into The Championships.

Back problems, which recurred when she played her first match for almost two months at the French Open, meant that after starting the year in magnificent form, her opening round match at Wimbledon was only her fifth since March.

mary PIERCE

conchita MARTINEZ

3

4

Mary Pierce (France)
Age: 25
Born: Montreal, Canada
World ranking: 3

Conchita Martinez (Spain)
Age: 28
Born: Monzon
World ranking: 4

Mary Pierce arrived at The Championships on a high. Two weeks earlier she had added to the Grand Slam title she won in Australia in 1995 by winning the French Open amid a tumultuous reception from a crowd which had not witnessed a lady champion of their own since Françoise Durr in 1967.

She has great presence on the court. Some will argue too much, inasmuch that she can spend so much time fixing her hair, flexing her neck and legs and putting in eyedrops with regularity at changeovers that she does not concentrate sufficiently on the tennis which then follows.

At her best though, especially with her forehand in full cry, she can be almost unplayable. This unpredictability has certainly not helped her at Wimbledon where in five previous visits she had not gone beyond the quarter finals.

This time, in keeping with her world ranking, she was given her highest seeding but there was always the risk that a player who had never looked totally at ease on grass, would still be unable to conquer those demons when her mind was still appreciating what she had so recently achieved at Roland Garros. An emotional letdown would not have been surprising.

This was proving to be Conchita Martinez's most profitable and rewarding year since 1994 when she became the first Spanish player to win the ladies' singles at Wimbledon, with a triumph that denied Martina Navratilova a tenth title.

Not only had she won the German Open in Berlin where she beat Martina Hingis among others but she had been runner-up in several other leading tournaments. These included Amelia Island and the French Open, after playing brilliantly to beat fellow Spaniard, Arantxa Sanchez-Vicario, in the semifinals while she also reached that penultimate round at the Australian Open.

It was a big leap forward again after both her form and her ranking had been disappointing for much of the three previous years in which she had won only three tournaments.

While lacking the strength of serve which increasingly seems necessary on all courts these days, her backhand passing shot is one of the most admired in the ladies' game, while away from the courts she excels in a variety of activities other than sporting. She is, for instance, something of a wine connoisseur.

venus WILLIAMS

monica SELES

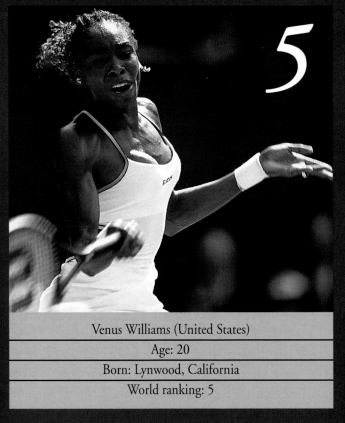

Venus Williams (United States)
Age: 20
Born: Lynwood, California
World ranking: 5

Monica Seles (United States)
Age: 26
Born: Novi Sad, Yugoslavia
World ranking: 6

The year did not start well for Venus Williams. The wrist injury, which she had suffered during the Chase Championships in New York in the previous November, showed no sign of healing quickly and her father Richard had suggested, in typically forthright fashion, that she might be wise to take a whole year away from tennis.

It was beginning to look as if that might be so when she was unable to return to the circuit until May, so the obvious fear for the 20-year-old was that she might not have had enough match practice in time to allow the power and vitality in her game to flow freely at The Championships.

At her peak, with her height and reach, supplementing the other match-winning characteristics in her game, many felt it would only be a matter of time before she was fit enough to become a Wimbledon champion.

In the two previous years she had gone so close to beating both Jana Novotna, who went on to win the title and then Steffi Graf — both in quarter finals which were among the best matches of the fortnight. All she needed was a touch more consistency and accuracy and her game would be a match for anyone.

Life has not always been easy for Monica Seles. The stabbing incident in Hamburg on 1 May 1993, when she was dominant at the top of the world rankings and had won seven of the previous eight Grand Slam titles in which she had competed, was a savage blow to her ambitions.

It was more than two years before the psychological scars healed sufficiently for her to return to the circuit but although within a matter of weeks she reached the final of the US Open and then won the Australian Open title four months later, somehow her game has never quite been the same.

The death in May 1998 of her father, who had coached her to the number one ranking, was another setback just when it looked as if she might once more be a major and regular challenger for the most important titles.

Yet Seles, who was runner-up at Wimbledon in 1992 but has never since gone beyond the quarter final in trying to win the only Grand Slam title which still eludes her, has never stopped working to improve her game. She is particularly renowned for those flaying double-fisted returns on both flanks, with or without the equally famous grunts.

nathalie TAUZIAT

serena WILLIAMS

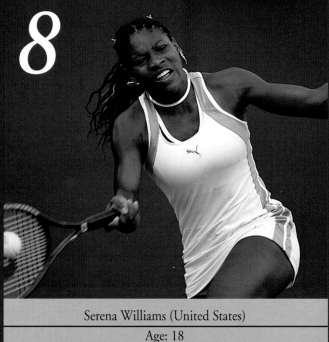

Nathalie Tauziat (France)
Age: 32
Born: Bangui, Central African Republic
World ranking: 7

Serena Williams (United States)
Age: 18
Born: Saginaw, Michigan
World ranking: 8

Nathalie Tauziat was making headlines in a big way all round the world in the four weeks leading into The Championships. The reason was her book which had just been published and which, according to some translations, was not likely to make her popular with many other players, including champions past and present. As for the player herself, who insisted that her words had not been translated accurately, her only concern was that she enjoyed one last impressive run at the tournament where she had achieved her most notable success during a 16-year career, by reaching the final in 1998.

There was every reason for such optimism. Earlier in the year she had reached a career-best fifth place on the world rankings and she knew that stylish touch and court craft contributed towards a game able to thrive on grass. On the other hand there had been signs in the weeks leading into Wimbledon that her pace about the court, which had helped her win Eastbourne in 1995 and establish an impressive record in the past in Birmingham, was beginning to falter under the increasing pressure of heavy hitters now in the game.

When Venus Williams was first allowed to test her strength on the WTA Tour, her father would often smile happily when others began forecasting great things for her and say 'You're right — but wait until you see Serena, she's going to be even better.'

That forecast, which seemed outrageously bold at the time, looked like being justified at the US Open last year when Serena powered her way into the final and then beat Martina Hingis, still exhausted from her huge battle with Venus in the semi-finals, for the title.

Apart from her strength, Serena appeared to have moved ahead of Venus in terms of developing an all-court game, especially when it came to taking charge of a rally from the net.

Like Venus, her progress in the first half of the year 2000 had been limited by injury and there had certainly been some demoralising setbacks along the way. Wimbledon, though, was the perfect inspiration for both of them. The only drawback was the possibility of them having to play each other in the semi-finals.

Above: The new Millennium Building.

*Opposite: Aerial view of The All England
Lawn Tennis & Croquet Club.*

WIMBLEDON

day **1**

MONDAY 26 JUNE

Above: A magnificent view of the new Millennium Building, which in turn offers members and (on the top floor) players an equally fine view of matches on No. 2 Court.

Opposite: Pete Sampras made a solid rather than spectacular start to his bid for a seventh singles title.

The first day of a new Wimbledon is always something of an adventure. It was especially so this time. All the boards and covers, which for the past two years had been masking where the popular but venerable No. 1 Court had been, were gone, revealing the magnificently modern new Millennium Building, which had been officially opened on the day of the draw by the President of the All England Club, HRH The Duke of Kent.

For the regulars it was rather like moving into a new home, and so far as the players, media and Club members were concerned, it was very much a day for finding their way around. For the public too, there was plenty which was new and improved among the facilities for them to explore and admire.

One Wimbledon feature, though, which never changes, providing the weather allows, is the invitation to the defending men's singles champion to launch the Centre Court programme and there was a warm welcome back for Pete Sampras, as he walked out to start at 2 p.m. precisely, against Jiri Vanek, a newcomer from the Czech Republic.

It was the start of an always-challenging road which he hoped would not only lead to his seventh Wimbledon crown but also his 13th Grand Slam title, which would enable him to pass the record he currently shared with Roy Emerson. The top seed, watched by fellow American Bridgette Wilson to whom he had become engaged a few days earlier, won comfortably, 6–4, 6–4, 6–2, delivering 15 aces in the process and then left no-one in any doubt about his continuing hunger for Grand Slam, especially Wimbledon titles.

Above: Vince Spadea's double-handed passing shots helped him end his sequence of 22 defeats as he created the biggest shock on the opening day by upsetting Britain's 14th-seeded Greg Rusedski (opposite).

Rusedski was drawn to face Vince Spadea, a talented American severely lacking in confidence, there had been forebodings. One day Spadea was going to end his record-breaking losing sequence of 22 matches stretching back to October 1999. Surely the big-serving Rusedski, though out of form himself, would not be that fall guy? Unhappily for the 26-year-old left-hander, he was.

Spadea had nothing to lose; Rusedski had the weight of the world on his shoulders at the one tournament where most British players want to impress. With the light fading earlier than one would expect in late June and storm clouds not far away, even the British fans in the Centre Court crowd struggled to offer him encouragement as he lost the first set.

Yet time and again courage and instinct kept Rusedski fighting for survival until in the end his shattered confidence, after weeks of failing to rediscover his match-winning serve, was his downfall. Four times he saved break points but just when it looked as if he might be playing himself fully through a nightmare, his nerves deserted him and he was beaten 6–3, 6–7, 6–3, 6–7, 9–7 in three hours 56 minutes.

Winning a break point for only the third time in 19 attempts, Rusedski found himself ahead for the first time as the contest, which at times was as gruesome as it was gripping, headed towards its fifth hour. His hopes, though, were instantly dashed. Starting with a double fault, his 15th, Rusedski hit two more errors as he served for what would have been a memorable triumph.

Instead those errors helped steady the equally shaky Spadea nerves for he held to lead 8–7 and then ended his eight months of despair when, on his fifth match point, his forehand was too powerful for Rusedski

'I'm very passionate about this place and would love to break the record here' he said. 'There are no guarantees I am going to win but it's going to take someone playing well to beat me.'

While it was plain sailing for Sampras, however, a body blow to British hopes was not far away. Somehow from the moment Greg

to control and the backhand volley dropped over the baseline.

'I tried my best' said a disconsolate Rusedski. 'I served for the match. I saved match points. I gave everything I could. I used to be able to finish off matches but when you're struggling with your form and confidence, that's the hardest part. And I'm struggling.'

Rusedski had been one of the four established grass court players promoted well above their rankings into seeded places along with Richard Krajicek, Pat Rafter and Mark Philippoussis. His defeat probably brought wry smiles from Alex Corretja and Albert Costa, the two Spaniards so affronted by being relegated that they withdrew from the tournament and returned home, although there was also the thought that with a Davis Cup semi-final on clay two weeks later, Wimbledon was not the only event on their mind. On the other side of the coin, though, former champion, Richard Krajicek, originally due to play Costa, overcame a slow start to outserve Germany's Michael Kohlmann 3–6, 6–1, 6–4, 7–6.

Rusedski was not the only men's seed to trip at the first hurdle. Nicolas Lapentti, who wanted all the grass court match time he could muster in readiness for leading Ecuador against Britain in a Davis Cup, World Group qualifying round match at Wimbledon one week after The Championships, was beaten by the wily Slava Dosedel from the Czech Republic, 6–3, 6–2, 0–6, 6–1.

The opening day is also a vital one for those British players who have been granted wild cards and there were heartening victories for two of them, Martin Lee, who recorded one of the biggest wins of his injury-interrupted career, and Louise Latimer.

Lee had held match point at The Championships for the two previous

'If you take away my serve, you cut off my left arm.'

Greg Rusedski after his serve again let him down as he was beaten on the opening day of The Championships.

Below: Compensation for British supporters on the first day as Worthing's Martin Lee played with admirable determination to reach the second round.

years but lost. This time he was determined not to be on the receiving end of a hat-trick, although it was only after three match points had escaped him that he produced a penetrative backhand to clinch his 6–2, 6–4, 7–6 victory over Costa Rican, Juan Antonio Marin, ranked 135 places above him.

After storming through the first set, Lee had found himself trailing 0–3 in the second before determinedly fighting his way back to

take it. He then showed even more strength and stubbornness when breaking back when his opponent was serving for the third set at 5–4.

Latimer also battled through in increasingly difficult conditions to beat the American, Holly Parkinson, 3–6, 6–3, 6–4. At one stage when the drizzle was making footholds difficult, Latimer asked for the match to be stopped and, much to her amazement, was booed. 'I can understand the crowd being restless. It's not nice when a good match has to stop but the court was getting dangerous. I was using all my strength not to fall over.'

The Warwickshire girl's next opponent would be 11th-seeded Anke Huber, who beat the Middlesex player, Jo Ward, 7–5, 6–2, only moments after Sussex's Julie Pullin had the dubious distinction of being the first British player to be beaten. Although she broke Natasha Zvereva in the first game of their match, the Belarusian generally had the extra power required and went on to win 6–4, 6–3.

Otherwise it was a gloomy day for the British players. Miles MacLagan, who had squandered three match points against Boris Becker 12 months earlier, demonstrated plenty of character as he took the first set from Canadian, Daniel Nestor, and later as he saved three match points at 5–1 down in the fourth. He won the next three games and forced four break points to draw level at 5–5 but Nestor's added experience at this level pulled him through 4–6, 7–6, 6–2, 6–4 on his fifth match point.

The years when none of the ladies entered the competition until Day 2 are long since gone, together now with net cord judges and coaches being allowed in the ladies locker room — a request made incidentally by the WTA Tour following a decision by the top players.

Although the tradition of the defending champion opening the Centre Court programme on Day Two remained, there was huge interest in the first day appearances of four of the game's most charismatic players and personalities, Martina Hingis, Anna Kournikova and the Williams sisters, Venus and Serena.

Returning to the No. 1 Court where she suffered a humiliating first round defeat by Jelena Dokic a year earlier, Hingis had obviously cast that miserable experience from her memory and stroked the ball around the court with her customary stylish mixture of skilful shots. She beat Spain's Angeles Montolio 6–1, 6–2, with most of the entertainment for the crowd coming when it took her nine match points to finish it off.

Separating the workmanlike Sampras and the fretting Rusedski on Centre Court was Kournikova,

Above: There was nothing to celebrate at the end of the day for these three British wild cards (left to right), Jo Ward, Julie Pullin and Miles MacLagan but the energetic, hard working Louise Latimer (below left) revived domestic spirits by rallying from a set down to beat the American, Holly Parkinson.

Anna Kournikova (left) showed plenty of style as she dismissed Sandrine Testud (below).

Opposite: Martina Hingis (top), in sharp contrast to the previous year, was all smiles as she made a winning start against Angeles Montolio (bottom).

whose exposure, if that is the right word, brings her more column inches — as well as some envious remarks from fellow players — than anyone else in the game. Still in search of the first title of her career, the Russian, just 19, had a potentially tricky opening match against the 10th-seeded French player, Sandrine Testud.

It was a lengthy, chilly and sometimes erratic match, interrupted for a while by the irritating drizzle. Kournikova was leading 6–5 when the covers had to go on. When she returned 75 minutes later, she quickly won the set and led 5–2 in the second before her game went to pieces and in next to no time they were into a third set.

Once more Kournikova led 5–2 but again her service games made nervous wrecks of her fans as Testud pulled back two games and had two chances to level at 5–5 but then floundered just as wastefully and the Russian pin-up held on to win 7–5, 5–7, 6–4 after two hours 15 minutes.

The draw had produced the enticing possibility of the Williams sisters having to meet in the semi-finals and it was immediately evident that, despite the problems both had suffered from injuries earlier in the year, they were very much back in business. 'Stay tuned, our fans will have a lot of action coming up. I feel confident and tournament tough' said younger sister, Serena, seeded eight, after dismissing Sweden's Asa Carlsson 6–3, 6–2.

Venus was just as effective, albeit with a few impetuous blunders thrown in, during a 6–3, 6–1 victory over Kveta Hrdlickova of the Czech Republic but a little more circumspect, not entirely sure that she had played enough tennis coming into The Championships to reach her peak in time. As we know now, she need not have worried.

With all due respect to Jan-Michael Gambill, few outside his own entourage arrived at the All England Club for the second day of The Championships expecting him to beat Lleyton Hewitt, the 19-year-old Australian thought by many to be the main obstacle to Pete Sampras once more retaining the title.

Yet beat him he did and in the most handsome, exhilarating style in straight sets. From his scorching first serve on the opening point which flew away off the outer frame of Hewitt's racket, Gambill, 23, launched a full-scale assault which seemed to catch his 19-year-old opponent off-guard.

Having been overpowered by Gambill's consistently stunning serves and blistering returns in the first two sets, the seventh seed eventually found the adrenalin which is such an essential part of his game to establish a 5–2 third-set lead. But it was still not enough for him to transform a mini-revival into a comprehensive one.

There were plenty of those familiar cries of 'C'mon' as Hewitt tried to whip himself into shape but there was far too little of the swashbuckling style which had helped carry him to victory over Sampras in the Stella Artois final nine days earlier.

'I just had one of those days' said Hewitt, who had suffered an equally disappointing letdown of form and confidence in his previous Centre Court appearance one year earlier, against three-times former champion, Boris Becker. 'It's a shame. You know you're going to have days like this but you just hope it happens in a small event rather than Wimbledon.'

While Hewitt was clearly not at his best, much of the responsibility for that was due to Gambill who has probably never played better than in the first two sets and then demonstrated admirable resolve under pressure in the third, instead of just letting that set slip away.

As Hewitt said 'He was not just hitting great returns but bombs.' Gambill's double-handed power off the ground on both flanks kept his opponent struggling and the crowd spellbound. He richly deserved the standing ovation which greeted the last in a long line of service winners and his 6–3, 6–2, 7–5 victory in two hours three minutes after boldly saving a break-back point in the final game with an ace.

While Hewitt's involvement was therefore restricted to the mixed doubles, double joy was developing for British fans as first the fast-improving Arvind Parmar and then Tim Henman, eager to justify his promotion to eighth place in the seedings, moved into the second round.

After the dramatic exit of Rusedski, the pressure on Henman as flagbearer for the home contingent had become all the greater but he kept his composure during a rampant first set by Thailand's

Left: Jan-Michael Gambill hails his magnificent first round victory over seventh-seeded Lleyton Hewitt, illustrated on the previous spread.

Below: A job well done by Tim Henman, after he had survived an explosive first set by Thailand's Paradorn Srichaphan.

'You really should try to rise above that instead of being a little childish and going home. It's a bit disappointing. This is the biggest event we have in the game and everybody should play.'

Pete Sampras on the decision by Spaniards Alex Corretja and Albert Costa to withdraw in protest at not being seeded.

Opposite: Perfect concentration from Arvind Parmar as he beat Andre Sa in the first round.

Below: Lancashire left-hander Barry Cowan fought hard to keep his match with American, Justin Gimelstob, alive overnight.

90th-ranked Paradorn Srichaphan, to win 5–7, 6–3, 6–1, 6–3.

With nothing to lose and knowing that Henman had yet to win a match on grass this year after losing in the first round of his two Wimbledon build-up tournaments, Srichaphan went freely for ferocious winners at every opportunity. Even Henman fans warmed to the spirit and approach of a little-known competitor, who clearly relished the opportunity and was cheered to the echo as he graciously bowed to all four sides of the court at the end.

One break in the 11th game settled the first set but Henman, whose shot selection and touch were always superior, took 12 out of 13 points in racing from 5–2 in the second set and thereafter was always in charge.

Parmar, who had upset Cedric Pioline in Nottingham a week earlier, played with admirable fortitude in twice recovering from a set down to beat the 23-year-old Brazilian, Andre Sa, 6–7, 6–3, 4–6, 6–2, 6–3, as he delighted an excited evening crowd packing every inch of space round Court 14.

The 6ft 4in Parmar, who had just reached a career-best 137 in the world rankings, certainly had to subdue an opponent who was reluctant to leave the baseline. It meant many of the rallies were more akin to those one normally watches on clay courts. But Parmar, who had also taken a set from Pete Sampras at Queen's Club was equally resilient and persistent with his firmly struck groundstrokes.

The turning point came in the sixth game of the fourth set when Parmar, whose footwork and mobility had also been sharpened, raced the full width of the court to deliver a spectacular passing winner on break point. From then on the 22-year-old from Hitchin held the initiative, although not without more anxious moments before he knew he would be playing Marc Rosset in the second round.

Serving for the match, Parmar faced a break point after a tentative second serve which received short shrift from Sa but he saved it with a cool backhand drop volley and went on to win when his opponent failed to return a backhand on the second match point.

Although Justin Gimelstob prevented

A combination of action — and anguish:
Andre Agassi (right) and Yevgeny
Kafelnikov (below) on their way to
respective first round victories over Phil
Dent (bottom left) and Roger Federer.

a British hat-trick of successes by curbing a noble fight back by Barry Cowan, who had snatched a third set tie-break in a match unfinished overnight, all this tended to overshadow the first appearance of former champion and world number one, Andre Agassi. Playing the third match of the day on Centre Court, Agassi made a sluggish start and lost the opening set against 19-year-old American qualifier Taylor Dent. Once he broke in the second, though, Agassi found the rhythm and timing he needed and was wholly in command by the time his limping opponent, son of the former Australian Davis Cup player, Phil Dent, had to stop because of a knee injury with the second seed leading 2–6, 6–3, 6–0, 4–0.

Elsewhere in the men's singles, the only other seed to fall apart from Hewitt was Nicolas Kiefer who lost a tense battle against fellow German, Tommy Haas, 5–7, 6–4, 6–2, 6–3. Yevgeny Kafelnikov was pushed hard in all three sets by the useful Swiss teenager, Roger Federer, 7–5, 7–5, 7–6 and although French Open champion, Gustavo Kuerten, dropped a tie-break set against Chris Woodruff, for most of the seeds it was a rewarding day at the office. None felt that more so than 12th-seeded Pat Rafter, who felt re-assured that his right shoulder, on which he had surgery eight months earlier, was now well enough restored for him to become a serious title contender.

Above: Gustavo Kuerten in pensive mood as he tried to come to terms with grass courts two weeks after his triumph on the clay at Roland Garros.

A trio of leading ladies (opposite) on their way to first round victories, Mary Pierce (top left), Jennifer Capriati and (below), Alexandra Stevenson.

Below: Pat Rafter (left) on his way to beating Britain's Jamie Delgado (right).

Rafter beat British wild card, Jamie Delgado, who did not play badly but the difference between them was probably best illustrated as the second set tie-break was reaching its climax. Rafter hit an ace to save a set point. Delgado promptly double-faulted to lose the set and was beaten 6–3, 7–6, 6–1.

Walking on to Centre Court for the first time as defending champion is an experience surpassed only by winning the title, according to Lindsay Davenport though her joy on this occasion was quickly turned to despair when Corina Morariu, not only her opponent but also the partner with whom she had won the doubles a year earlier, collapsed in agony and had to default.

Davenport, still not entirely convinced about her own fitness after damaging her back at the French Open, was leading 6–3, 1–0, when Morariu damaged her knee and shoulder as she fell when wrong-footed by a Davenport forehand.

Seeding upsets in the first round of the ladies' singles are usually few but on this particular day only five of the nine in action survived, among them Monica Seles, Mary Pierce and former champion, Conchita Martinez. It was a particularly disappointing day for the French, with Julie Halard-Decugis, Nathalie Tauziat and Amélie Mauresmo, all failing to reach the second round, while Belgium's Dominique Van Roost, seeded 16, was well beaten 6–2, 6–4 by Jennifer Capriati.

Against that, however, Van Roost's fellow Belgian, Kim Clijsters, who had reached the fourth round a year earlier when she was only 16, sustained the promise shown then by outlasting Tauziat, the highest ranked among the beaten French trio, 6–3, 3–6, 6–2.

A grim day for the seeds as Richard Krajicek (right), Cedric Pioline (below) and the upended Magnus Norman (bottom) all suffered second round losses.

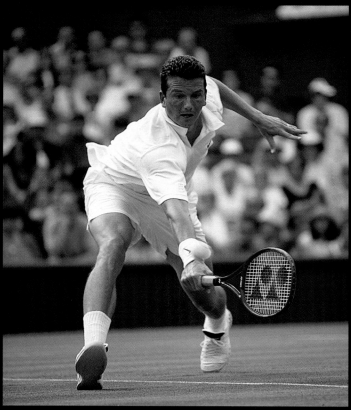

It was a day of drama and controversy wherever one looked — especially on the two leading courts. By the end of the day, The Championships had lost, at least from the singles, the most photographed tennis player of the year, Anna Kournikova, former champions Richard Krajicek and Conchita Martinez, as well as third-seeded Magnus Norman, and Pete Sampras had been taken to hospital. And that was only a taste of the excitement.

While a bitterly disappointed Kournikova knew her dream of winning the first title of her life in the one place where it would make the most impact had been destroyed by the French player Anne-Gaelle Sidot 6–3, 6–4 — 'she played very well and I made too many mistakes' — was her apt summing up of the match, Sampras's record breaking ambitions were hanging in the balance.

On a day when the top half of the draw opened up for him so invitingly, not only with the defeat of Krajicek and Norman but also sixth-seeded Cedric Pioline, his joy at surviving a second-round late-night thriller against Karol Kucera was countered by worry over a lower leg injury sustained midway through a two-hour 54-minute encounter. 'Sampras is suffering from an inflamed foot and will be having a scan in hospital tonight and his fitness will be evaluated in the morning' said a tournament spokesman.

It was while building a 5–1 lead in the third set that Sampras, who had only won the first set tie-break 11–9, began coming in gingerly behind his serve and, at 5–2, after a distracting alarm bell had added to the tension, he sent for the trainer. His leg was heavily strapped around and just above the left ankle.

For a while he looked to be in serious difficulty. One even wondered if he might be forced to stop. Yet he continued to produce spectacular serves — to save having to move too much — whenever Kucera was threatening to undermine him with equally telling returns.

Despite his obvious discomfort,

Sampras saved two break points in the second game of the fourth set and two more to avoid trailing 2–4. Kucera then double-faulted to go 3–4 down but still saved three match points in an amazing last game in which the defending champion also prompted renewed doubts

Below: Tears were shed as Anna Kournikova again failed to make a major impact in the ladies' singles.

Opposite: The first indication that Pete Sampras was in trouble with his inflamed foot as he receives treatment (opposite) from trainer, Doug Spreen but he still managed to beat Karol Kucera (bottom left). Olivier Rochus (bottom right) scored the best win of his life against Magnus Norman, while brilliant returning from Wayne Ferreira (below) knocked out former champion, Richard Krajicek.

about his suspect back by double-faulting three times. It was 9.08 p.m. when the Centre Court crowd, still almost at a capacity level, rose to acclaim Sampras's 7–6, 3–6, 6–3, 6–4 escape. His injury, it transpired, had first been evident during practice a few hours earlier. In a day of sparkling tennis, the shock results and another row involving Jeff Tarango, by far the biggest surprise was the 6–4, 2–6, 6–4, 6–7, 6–1 defeat of Norman, runner-up at the French Open, by Olivier Rochus, a 19-year-old

Belgian qualifier competing in his first Grand Slam.

Rochus, whose elder brother, Christophe, 21, was also still in the tournament, waiting to play a second round match he was to lose against Holland's Sjeng Schalken, impressed with his magnificent groundstrokes and coolness under pressure. His was a remarkable tale inasmuch that it was only at the last minute that he decided to enter the qualifying. Norman went into the match with a 42–12 match record for the year but was frequently beaten by the sheer pace of the returns and passes by an opponent modestly placed at 179 on the entry system.

When Norman levelled in the second set, the general assumption was that his extra experience would turn the match round. Instead Rochus, junior doubles champion with Roger Federer two years earlier, lifted his game to an even greater level.

While Jan-Michael Gambill was unleashing more of his thunderous groundstrokes to beat Fabrice Santoro, 4–6, 6–4, 6–2, 6–2 — though not so consistently spectacular as against Lleyton Hewitt in the first round — Wayne Ferreira was in similarly ferocious form. He was especially impressive with his explosive returns as he upset Krajicek, the only man to beat Sampras at Wimbledon in the seven previous years on his way to the title in 1996, 5–7, 6–3, 6–3, 7–6.

Not that it was entirely plain sailing for the South African. Serving to keep the opening set alive at 5–6, Ferreira clashed verbally with umpire Kim Craven about an over-rule on set point and continued to swear after smashing his racket against his courtside chair when the set was lost. Ferreira, who was later fined, admitted that by sustaining his complaints in the way he did, he might even have been defaulted.

Instead he calmed down, allowed his racket to do the talking as Krajicek's serving became shaky and continued to open up the court with his first return before completing the point with his second shot.

Vladimir Voltchkov, the qualifier from Belarus (opposite top) continued to impress by beating former finalist, Cedric Pioline (below) while Martina Hingis (opposite bottom) succeeded as her boyfriend, Magnus Norman, failed on Day Three.

For Vladimir Voltchkov of Belarus, who upset the 1997 runner-up, Pioline, on Court Three, it was not the first time he had scored an impressive victory against the odds at The Championships. Voltchkov, 21, the junior boys' singles champion four years earlier, also beat Karol Kucera, then the 15th seed, in

1998. He took full advantage of Pioline's lethargy and erratic serving, which included four aces in the game which cost him the second set, for a fully deserved 6–3, 6–3, 2–6, 3–6, 6–4 victory in two hours 52 minutes.

Not for the first time, either, Tarango was booed off a Wimbledon court, although this time it was by no means such a stormy incident as in 1995 when he walked off, refusing to continue the match after a furious row with French umpire, Bruno Rebeuh, who was later attacked on site by the player's wife.

Tarango's target on this occasion was not umpire Gerry Armstrong, with whom he shook hands at the end, but opponent Paul Goldstein, a fellow graduate of Stanford University. Goldstein, who won 3–6, 6–2, 5–7, 6–2, 12–10, had called for the trainer when Tarango would be serving next at 9–10. He alleged this was gamesmanship and told Goldstein so in no uncertain terms when refusing to shake hands with him.

Goldstein seemed shocked by the suggestion and insisted 'I did nothing wrong or unethical' but Tarango said 'Of course he was faking the injury. He was running like a deer. He couldn't have been that injured.'

With Kournikova no longer involved, the focus in the ladies' singles concentrated even more on those most heavily tipped to be around for the final and all of them were in good form. Martina Hingis beat Jing-Qian Yi of China 6–4, 6–1, playing on the court alongside that where Hingis's boyfriend, Magnus Norman was being beaten. 'I didn't want to watch too much of his match before I went on court because I get too nervous. Unfortunately he lost but I had a good day at the office.'

Ai Sugiyama, ranked 20 in the world, produced more than enough elegant and effective shots to please the crowd on No. 1 Court but never had the strength to counter enough of the free-wheeling power flowing from Venus Williams's racket as she skipped happily to a 6–1, 6–4 victory. Her youngster sister, Serena,

Above: The unmistakable power in the Serena Williams serve as she took only 35 minutes to win in the second round.

Opposite: Anke Huber (top) was pushed hard most of the way to overcome Britain's Louise Latimer (bottom).

was even more impressive, giving Dutch qualifier, Yvette Basting what some people accurately but unchivalrously called a pasting, 6–1, 6–0 in a mere 35 minutes.

There was no evidence that the shortage of match practice by the Williams sisters was in any way inhibiting their progress and Serena gave ample notice of what was going through her mind when she said 'I was out for two months before the US Open last year but bounced back to win it.'

Venus and Serena are two of the tallest, as well as the strongest players on the ladies' circuit. One of the tiniest, 5ft 2in Canadian, Sonia Jeyaseelan, demonstrated that size does not always matter as she tormented Conchita Martinez to such an extent that the fourth-seeded former champion, was made to look a novice.

Jeyaseelan was so small when she first fell in love with tennis that she could not hold a racket with one hand. Her father, Reggie, a native of Sri Lanka, was so keen to deflect her from her ice skating ambitions on to the professional tennis road

that he moulded her into a two-handed player on both flanks. 'It may look ugly but it worked for me today' she enthused after romping to an unexpectedly comfortable 6–4, 6–1 victory to the astonishment of the crowd on Court Two.

There was no such pleasure for Britain's Martin Lee on the same court. Although he kept serving and returning well enough to take the first set from Moroccan, Younes El Aynaoui, number 16 in the world, once he was broken at the start of the second set his challenge evaporated and he was beaten 6–7, 6–2, 6–2, 6–2. The first set lasted 62 minutes, the other three a mere 64.

British fans on that court could hear excited cries also coming from Court 13 where Louise Latimer took the first set from Anke Huber, the vastly more experienced 11th-seeded German, ranked 108 places above her, but as in Lee's match the initiative could not be sustained. 'It was a very big chance for me but she was much more positive after the first set and I was always on the back foot' the plucky Latimer confessed.

Tim Henman is shown at full stretch in the previous spread on his way to beating Arnaud Clement.

Below: No-one could accuse Martin Damm of not bending his knees or not keeping the racket head up as he delivered one of his many winning low volleys to upset Marat Safin.

Never has there been such carnage of the seeds. Two more were knocked out in both the men's and ladies' singles, leaving only seven of the original 16 in the third round by the end of the fourth day. The victims included Mary Pierce, third seed in her event and fifth-seeded Yevgeny Kafelnikov among the men though neither was really quite the surprise it seemed at the time.

Kafelnikov, who has won Grand Slam titles in France and Australia, is notoriously unpredictable and strained muscles in the right shoulder hardly boosted either his confidence or concentration as he was beaten 6–1, 7–6, 6–4 by Sweden's Thomas Johansson. The Russian, who began the match with the first of his 11 double faults, called for the trainer after hitting another four, three of them in succession, to go 6–5 down in the second set by which time, he admitted, he was 'pretty close to quitting'.

He said that he had started feeling really sharp pains in his shoulder which made it almost impossible for him to lift his arm to go into his service action when he was 5–3 down in that set. One of the main reasons why he played on was because he had been forced to quit injured at Wimbledon the previous year and 'didn't want to go out on such a negative note again'.

Although he broke back after receiving treatment to force a tie-break, he lost it 7–0 and the shoulder — and therefore the serve — let him down again when he first served in the third set.

Kafelnikov's understudy as the number one Russian player, 15th-seeded Marat Safin, was also brought down to earth as he was beaten by Martin Damm of the Czech Republic. Safin, who was being coached during the short but important grass court season by former British Davis Cup player and coach, Tony Pickard, started well enough but then lost his way badly on his returns and was beaten 7–5, 7–6, 6–3. Damm could hardly believe his good fortune as Safin, instead of punishing mid-court and other shots which ought to have been put away, kept overhitting on his returns and volleys until he also lost patience with himself. He incurred a warning for ball abuse and flirted with another when he smashed his racket on the ground.

As Damm said, 'It's always good if you can see your opponent is in that sort

The pictures tell their own story. A dejected Marat Safin (left), beaten by Martin Damm, while Yevgeny Kafelnikov's injured shoulder (below left) hastened his defeat by Thomas Johansson (below).

Gustavo Kuerten (opposite) in full cry.

Todd Woodbridge (below) gave fellow Australian Pat Rafter a useful second round work-out. Todd Martin (bottom left) waits for an Andre Agassi lob to drop while it is a case of the long and the short of it as umpire Bruno Rebeuh greets 5ft 9in Michael Chang before his defeat by 6ft 7in Alexander Popp (bottom right).

of condition. I just kept telling myself to stay focused and to keep making him play. And whenever he missed a first serve, I was ready to try taking advantage on the second.'

In a fascinating match on Court 2, Pat Rafter's serve just gave him the edge against the often brilliant returns by fellow Australian, Todd Woodbridge. The exchanges were often swift, penetrating and skilful, giving Rafter exactly the challenge he needed for tougher battles to come. He won 6–3, 6–3, 6–4, but the first set in particular was closer than the score suggested.

On the adjoining Court 3, French Open champion, Gustavo Kuerten's groundstrokes again flowed freely as he stopped a worthy bid by Justin Bower, the left-handed South African qualifier, 6–4, 6–4, 7–5. Kuerten's next task was to be against Germany's Alexander Popp, whose possession of a British passport through his mother, who was born in Wolverhampton, was exciting those who viewed him as another possible British import.

Popp, 6ft 7in, regained his composure well after missing chances to take the third set as he registered a splendid

7–6, 4–6, 6–7, 6–3, 8–6 triumph over Michael Chang, whose relative lack of height (5ft 9in) was underlined every time they passed one another at the net.

This was also one of those all-too-frequent days at Wimbledon 2000 when tournament referee Alan Mills and his staff, not to mention the public, were extremely lucky that the weather did not cause the delays which had seemed likely. There were only momentary glimpses of a patch of blue in the sky to remind us that it was supposed to be summer but it was not until late in the evening that a combination of drizzle and bad light interrupted the play.

One of the matches which remained unfinished overnight involved Andre Agassi and fellow American Todd Martin and Agassi, with his heavy fall on a slippery court at Queen's Club, was not happy with Mr Mills for not calling a halt earlier to what was developing into an exciting match.

It was only after Agassi, reacting like a soccer player trying to win a free kick, had gone into an exaggerated fall that play was stopped at 30–30 in the second game of the fourth set. The former champion was leading 6–4, 2–6, 7–6,

Arnaud Clement (below) was always under pressure from Tim Henman.

Opposite: Jelena Dokic (top left) powers to victory, while Lindsay Davenport (top right) clenches her first in delight after beating Elena Likhovtseva (bottom right). Magui Serna (bottom left) kept her eye on the ball well enough to beat French Open champion Mary Pierce.

0–1 at the time and the Centre Court clock stood at 8.28 p.m. as the drizzle started to become appreciably heavier.

'Why are you out here now. Why didn't you call it off before? It's not right. People could get injured out here' snapped the angry former champion although next morning, when he calmed down, he telephoned the referee's office to apologise for losing his temper.

One player who just beat the weather was Mark Philippoussis, who recovered from losing the first set against Frenchman, Arnaud Di Pasquale, but then stepped up the tempo for a convincing 4–6, 7–6, 6–3, 6–0 victory just as players on all other courts were being called off for the night.

It may not have been spectacular, but Tim Henman's performance was certainly efficient as he moved into the third round at the expense of Frenchman, Arnaud Clement. 'Very satisfying' was how Henman described his 6–4, 6–4, 6–4 victory in two hours 8 minutes which prompted the waving of Union Jack flags all round Centre Court.

At a time when other seeds were disappearing at such a rapid rate, Henman looked secure from the moment he broke his 22-year-old opponent, although it was also a match in which he could ill-afford to take extravagant risks — and he knew it.

Clement, whose emotions were hidden behind wrap-around sunglasses which he wears even for indoor matches, occasionally looked a figure of fun when he found himself trapped so close to the net that he wisely stuck the racket up in front of his nose for protection. Yet as Henman discovered through the accuracy and skill of Clement's passing shots, the man who had survived 30 aces in beating a now disconsolate Goran Ivanisevic in the first round had to be taken seriously.

'I had to work very hard out there' said Henman. 'On the two occasions I lost my serve it was because I didn't put in enough first serves and he pounced straight away. I knew I needed to maintain the consistency in all aspects of my game to remain in control.'

Henman thus became the sole British player in the third round for, after hanging on grimly through a first set which was decided by one mini-break in a tie-break, Arvind Parmar's resistance started to ebb away and he was beaten 7–6, 7–5, 6–3 by the relentless power serving of Swiss veteran, Marc Rosset, on Court 18.

Devon's Lucie Ahl, who had amply justified her wild card by beating Austria's Barbara Schwartz in the opening round, battled hard but was unable to sustain it in the second as she went down 6–4, 6–3 to Sandra Nacuk of Yugoslavia, ranked more than 100 places above her.

A little more than two weeks after being crowned champion at Roland Garros, Mary Pierce was unable to lift herself either physically or emotionally to make a full-blooded attempt for further success on a surface where her footwork and mobility remain suspect.

Having moved swiftly to a 3–0 lead in the first set, Pierce relaxed and then struggled to retain the mastery over the tigerish Magui Serna from Spain and she was beaten in two tie-breaks.

It was by no means easy either for Lindsay Davenport who, 12 months after winning the title, teetered on the brink for a while before lifting her game just in time to beat Elena Likhovtseva of Russia, 3–6, 6–3, 6–3. Four times in the final set the challenger had a point to lead 4–0 but Davenport survived to break back and then raced through the next five games.

Arantxa Sanchez-Vicario and Monica Seles continued to make progress towards what could be a fascinating fourth round clash but so did one of the leading new generation players, Jelena Dokic, 17, a quarter finalist in 1999. She refused to be distracted by her father's brush with a television reporter, which led to the police being called and professionally went about her business with a 7–6, 6–1 defeat of Spain's Gala Leon Garcia.

All in all it was quite a day.

Todd Martin made no bones about it. It was 1996 all over again as his self-belief agonisingly deserted him while he was holding what looked like a winning lead on the Centre Court before he allowed Andre Agassi to remain a prime candidate for the men's singles title.

Four years earlier Martin, now 29, stood one game away from a place in the final when he led another fellow American, Mali Vai Washington 5–1 in the final set of their rain-delayed semi-final and lost 10–8. This time he held a 5–2 double-break advantage in the final set of their second round clash interrupted overnight by the weather, only to be punished for a sudden bout of errors 37 minutes after missing the first of his two match points. Once again defeat came in the 18th game of the fifth.

Agassi, who must have been surprised, as well as relieved, to have survived 6–4, 2–6, 7–6, 2–6, 10–8, was being just as honest and frank as his disappointed opponent when he said: 'You need a little help from 2–5 down and I was very lucky to get back into the match. When I lost my serve a second time [in the final set], I didn't think there was a lot of help left but I was determined to make him work to serve out for it. So great things can still happen' he added. And if they had done so, it would have been the first time since 1960, when Neale Fraser beat Butch Buchholz that a champion would have saved one or more match points along the way. As we now know, Fraser's record remains intact.

Martin had been serving so impressively, with at least one ace in almost every service game after play resumed from its overnight break, with him serving at 30–30 for a 2–0 lead in the fourth set that his failure, not just once but twice to serve out for the match, was so surprising.

'I really felt I had got to the point where I was controlling play' said Martin. 'Since he broke me twice in the first

Opposite: Andre Agassi took the chances he was offered to escape from 2–5 down in the final set by fellow American, Todd Martin (below).

Below: Olivier Rochus, the giant-killer from the second round, was outwitted in the third round by the added experience of veteran Italian, Gianluca Pozzi (opposite).

set, I didn't get broken again until I was leading 5–2 in the fifth... The tide can turn very quickly. I hit an ace on the first point at 5–2 but he did a good return to make it 15–15 and before you knew it I was between a rock and a hard place. Once that happens, once one of those breaks go, the other guy gets a bit of a boost. Also it's tough for the server to come back if he has to serve again and try and play a good game with those vivid memories' he added wistfully.

One of the problems for a player who knocks out a seed in the early rounds of a Grand Slam is that they then probably find themselves being challenged by Tour journeyman not unlike themselves, so a sense of anti-climax must be a risk. That was not so, however, for Wayne Ferreira, Jan-Michael Gambill or Belarusian qualifier, Vladimir Voltchkov, as

they moved into the fourth round. Joy in the Belgian corner of the media room, though, after Olivier Rochus, both the youngest and smallest player in the men's singles, saw off third-seeded Magnus Norman, vanished abruptly with his 6–3, 3–6, 7–6, 6–2 defeat by the oldest — and one of the canniest — 35-year-old Italian, Gianluca Pozzi.

All this had been a new experience for Rochus. Not so with Ferreira, who can look back on five Wimbledons when he has been seeded and knocked out by someone not rated so highly and three times when he has been the unseeded slayer of a seed. He did not start convincingly against the Romanian, Andrei Pavel on Court 18 but once into his heavy hitting stride, he polished off a worthily stubborn opponent 3–6, 7–6, 7–5, 6–3.

When Gambill walked on to No. 1 Court to face fellow American, Paul Goldstein, it was a far cry from their junior boys days when they met in the final of the US National Boys Singles in 1994, with Goldstein winning in straight sets.

Since then Goldstein has obtained a degree in human biology and Gambill, apart from acquiring a fabulous collection of vintage and classic Jaguar cars, had moulded his game round a big serve and even more ferocious returns and passes to become the next in line in America for Davis Cup selection.

The first set was as thrilling as Gambill's first round match with Lleyton Hewitt, with two well-matched and athletic players sustaining lengthy rallies before Gambill snatched the tie-break and then moved on rather more easily than he may have expected to a 7–6 6–2, 6–2 victory.

Voltchkov followed up his first round defeat of the sixth-seeded Cedric Pioline with a 7–6, 7–5, 7–6 defeat of Younes El Aynaoui, who would have been the 16th seed had they been based solely on world listings. There was just one service break in the 12th game of the second set when the Moroccan double-faulted on the only break point he had faced in the match. The tenacious Voltchkov, again covering the court with a confidence and relish many would envy, had underlined his coolness by saving eight break points in the first set.

Also through to the fourth round went Sweden's Jonas Bjorkman, equalling his best performance at The Championships and Byron Black of Zimbabwe, for whom it would mean a first appearance in the last 16. Pete Sampras's third round match with Justin Gimelstob was postponed until the following day when rain set in just as the evening crowd was arriving. They would have been disappointed but not so Sampras, who would be able to rest his injured foot a little longer before meeting his fellow American.

By the same token Venus Williams's third round match with Nathalie Dechy of France was held over but Serena Williams beat the rain, which temporarily forced her off court after only 15 minutes of her meeting with Spain's Cristina Torrens-Valero, by racing on to a 6–2, 6–1 victory once they returned to the court, in only 45 minutes.

It was the second time in the week

Paul Goldstein (opposite) began well enough but lost his way against fellow American, Jan-Michael Gambill, while Jonas Bjorkman (below) was naturally delighted to equal his best previous performance at Wimbledon by reaching the fourth round.

Below: Delight for some lucky fans as Martina Hingis provides them with autographs after moving comfortably into the last 16 against Silvija Talaja.

that Martina Hingis, who was expecting to face Serena in the semi-finals, always assuming she would not trip up against Venus in the quarters, had been thwarted in her efforts to run the rule over the 18-year-old by the speed of her victory. 'She must be playing pretty well' said Hingis, who was also reasonably content with her own progress as she beat Silvija Talaja, up to 22 in the world, 6–2, 6–2. The impressive Croatian had pushed Hingis hard on the clay in Berlin in May but this time she kept squandering service games when apparently in control. Twice in the second set she was broken from 40–0 and Hingis was quick to take advantage.

Hingis's next opponent would be Germany's Anke Huber, who was the first through to the last 16 when she beat Slovakia's Tina Pisnik 6–2, 6–3. Meanwhile Lisa Raymond reached the second week for the fourth time in her career with an easy 6–2, 6–1 win over the Canadian, Sonya Jeyaseelan, who showed little of the form which upset Conchita Martinez one round earlier.

Olga Barabanschikova also came through impressively against Amy Frazier and Thailand's Tamarine Tanasagarn was a 6–1, 4–6, 6–4 victor over the French player, Anne-Gaelle Sidot, who then went into the interview room to refute allegations of racism levelled against her earlier in the week by Alexandra Stevenson.

She called the allegations, which had been fully investigated and dismissed by the WTA, 'a lie'.

Left: *No doubting how much these fans love Wimbledon, as they take a general look over the Southern side of the grounds (below).*

Almost 70 years of Wimbledon history is encapsulated in the wonderful gathering of former champions overleaf, including John McEnroe, Boris Becker and Pat Cash who are highlighted (inset).

Opposite: the emotional parade of champions including, left to right, from the top, Bunny Austin, Sidney Wood, Frank Sedgman, Ken Rosewall, Neale Fraser, Angela Mortimer Barrett, Maria Bueno, Margaret Court, Roy Emerson, Manuel Santana, Stan Smith, Billie Jean King, Ann Jones, Virginia Wade, Evonne Goolagong Cawley, Bjorn Borg, Chris Evert, Martina Navratilova, Steffi Graf and Stefan Edberg.

Below: Rod Laver is presented with his memento of the occasion, a Waterford Crystal plate, by The Duchess of Gloucester, Honorary President of The Lawn Tennis Association.

Increasingly in recent years, a major talking point among many of those arriving at Wimbledon each day, once they have scanned the Order of Play to know which matches they are likely to see, has been the weather. On days four and five especially, the 42 acres of the All England Club were largely spared the rain which had been forecast and had been falling only a few miles away.

Seldom, then, had everyone been keeping their fingers crossed more earnestly than on this sixth day when almost 70 years of Wimbledon history were to be represented by 64 former singles and multiple doubles champions in a Centre Court parade to mark the new millennium.

Even the Press Box was filled almost to capacity — usually the journalists are spread far and wide round the courts until the latter stages of The Championships — as tennis heroes and heroines dating back to 1931 men's singles winner, Sidney Wood, proudly returned to the scene of their greatest sporting triumphs.

The prolonged standing ovation when they first appeared was clearly as emotional for some of them as it was for the crowd. One by one they took their individual bows as they were greeted by The Duchess of Gloucester, Honorary

President of The Lawn Tennis Association and presented with a personalised engraved plate.

Chris Evert, whose three victories spanned 1974–1981, called it 'a humbling experience' to be with so many of the great players from the past 'who played just for the love of the sport and did not enjoy the financial benefits in the way my own and later generations have done.'

Memories of some of Wimbledon's greatest matches flooded back as the parade, led by the track-suited Andre Agassi, who then had to dash away to prepare for a match, began. One of the most ecstatic welcomes went to Bunny Austin, the last surviving British men's singles finalist from 1938 who, approaching his 94th birthday, was determined to take part even though it meant him being in a wheelchair.

Among other obvious favourites were Billie Jean King, Rod Laver, Evonne Goolagong Cawley, Chris Evert, Martina Navratilova, Steffi Graf, Boris Becker, Stefan Edberg, the three British lady champions, Angela Mortimer Barrett, Ann Jones and Virginia Wade plus, probably most of all, Bjorn Borg and John McEnroe.

It was the first time they had been together at The Championships since McEnroe ended Borg's extraordinary achievement of winning the five consecutive men's singles titles in 1981. Their 18–16 tie-break a year earlier, which Borg lost although he still went on to win the match, has became part of tennis legend. Others, like Pete Sampras, waiting to play the first match on Centre Court and the doubles champions, Mark Woodforde and Todd Woodbridge, already playing on an outside court, were later presented between matches in the Royal Box.

Tim Henman, who even delayed his practice session until after he had seen Borg, his boyhood hero, saluted by the crowd, said the parade made it 'a special day'. It was simply and brilliantly that — and the matches which followed lived

up to the tradition — as well as a glorious occasion.

As the former champions gathered in the Royal Box so Sampras, arguably the finest grass court player of all time, took his place in front of them against fellow United States Davis Cup player, Justin Gimelstob. The main question was Sampras's fitness. At first that remained in doubt. He was cautious, with no real zip in his play as his 94th-ranked opponent took the first set 6–2 in 24 minutes.

The longer Gimelstob was able to deliver bombing serves and keep Sampras on the back foot, the greater the possibility of a shock but then suddenly at 4–4, 30–30, the master produced a great running return winner, which was the signal for his recovery. Although Gimelstob saved the first break point, Sampras, immediately looking as if a great weight had been lifted from his shoulders, struck a winning service return down the line and then an equally stylish backhand pass for a break which sped him on to a 2–6, 6–4, 6–2, 6–2 victory.

Over on Court One, Andre Agassi was maintaining predictable, though sometimes surprisingly erratic, progress with a 6–3, 6–3, 6–4 win over French left-hander Jerome Golmard while 12th-seeded Pat Rafter was maintaining his renewed enthusiasm with a thorough enough 6–2, 7–6 (7–2), 6–3 defeat of Germany's Rainer Schuttler. That made the Australian the only survivor in the bottom half of the draw yet to concede a set.

The principal seeding upset of the day came when French Open champion, Gustavo Kuerten, suffering from a chest infection, was unable to stem the flow of heavy serves and equally formidable groundstrokes emanating from the racket of 6ft 7in German, Alexander Popp.

As he basked in 'probably the nicest day of my life up to now' after winning 7–6 (8–6), 6–2, 6–1, Popp, who had rarely attracted attention on previous tournament appearances in Britain, admitted that the issue of whether he

might play Davis Cup for Britain one day, rather than Germany, had been discussed but he was eager to keep it under control.

'Maybe some people think I'm trying to get into British tennis or something but I'm not really doing that' he insisted, as he then had to contemplate a fourth round clash with the only other 6ft 7in player in the tournament, Switzerland's Marc Rosset, who had beaten Popp's

Justin Gimelstob (opposite) threw everything he had into his match with Pete Sampras (below) but the top seed steadily regained control after losing the first set.

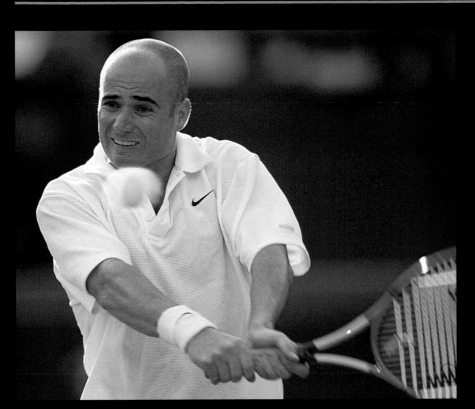

Storming on, Alexander Popp (opposite) against Gustavo Kuerten, Andre Agassi (left) against Jerome Golmard and Pat Rafter (below) against Rainer Schuttler.

For the second successive year, Sjeng Schalken (top) played — and lost — the longest men's singles match of the fortnight.

Mark Philippoussis (opposite) kept huffing and puffing until he wore the Dutchman down.

countryman, Tommy Haas, 6–4, 3–6, 6–3, 3–6, 9–7.

Henman, clearly inspired by the lunchtime parade, made sure he was never under more than token pressure from the gifted but mercurial Moroccan, Hicham Arazi, on Centre Court, by clamping his authority at the earliest opportunity — and then firmly maintaining his grip to win 6–3, 6–3, 6–3.

All that he needed to do then was to discover who his fourth round opponent 48 hours later would be. It was a long wait. Indeed when Mark Philippoussis walked back into the locker room after outlasting Holland's Sjeng Schalken 4–6, 6–3, 6–7, 7–6, 20–18 in five hours five minutes, Henman simply could not resist asking 'What took you so long?'

'They were just starting their fifth set

when I went out for my match and when I came back I could hardly believe that they were still playing' said the Oxfordshire player, now living in London.

Philippoussis, who served 44 aces, insisted that he would be more than ready to face Henman two days later and as if to emphasise the point, went into some jogging exercises. Certainly his mental resources seemed endless for Schalken twice looked to have the upper hand, especially when he pounded his way with several of his 30 aces, to take the third set tie-break 9–7.

Yet with several great former Australian champions supporting him from the members' box — Rod Laver, Margaret Court, Neale Fraser and Tony Roche among others — Philippoussis not only levelled in the fourth set but successfully served to stay in the match without allowing Schalken a single set point, no less than 14 times. Indeed the

only hint of his serve wavering in the final set came in the final game, though then only for two points.

There was some unfinished business from the night before in the ladies' singles, although Venus Williams, despite easing off in the second set, continued to play in a manner which was steadily reducing the odds against her as she completed third round matches in the top half of the draw with a 6–0, 7–6 defeat of France's Nathalie Dechy.

Courts 18 and 13 were the places to be for devotees of ladies' tennis, with players representing both the old and the new featuring successfully on these outside show courts which provide free access to everyone once they are in the grounds. On Court 18, Arantxa Sanchez-Vicario and the chunky Yugoslav teenager, Sandra Nacuk, played almost entirely from the baseline, from which both delivered returns and attempted passes with considerable ferocity.

Nacuk won the first set and even had two match points at 5–4 in the second before lack of experience led to a touch of nerves and a double fault on the first of them as Sanchez, 28, survived in the

tie-break and went on to a 3–6, 7–6, 6–2 victory.

On Court 13, Jelena Dokic, 17, took a couple of games to get into her stride but then dropped only two of the last 13 games as she raced to a 6–2, 6–1 defeat of the American, Brie Rippner in just 44 minutes. 'At 30–30 in the third game I told myself that the next game would be the one where I needed to break' said the increasingly mature Dokic. 'I knew if I could do that I'd be on top of her and on top of my game. That's what I did.'

There was also a hat-trick of successes in this half of the draw for Americans, with Lindsay Davenport, Monica Seles and Jennifer Capriati all making their expected progress to the last 16, although Capriati trailed 5–2 in the first set before beating Indonesia's Yayuk Basuki, 7–6, 6–0 on Court 3. She complained that the military band, entertaining the Centre Court crowd before the parade of champions, was upsetting her. Basuki's annoyance was not directed at the band but at the timing of Capriati's protest which she felt ruined her concentration.

'He's the greatest athlete we have ever seen in men's tennis. He didn't need to say anything but he had an aura. I don't think I've seen anything quite like that since he retired.'

John McEnroe talking about Bjorn Borg.

Venus Williams (opposite) found herself in a tougher than expected second set battle against Nathalie Dechy. It was even tougher for Arantxa Sanchez-Vicario (left) before she overcame the Yugoslavian, Sandra Nacuk in three sets.

No.1 Court
Courts 14 - 19

Aorangi Picnic Terrace
Large Screen TV

Ticket ReSale
Shops

Exit Gate 13
Buses To Wimbledon
Taxis

Court 2
Lost Property

Court 3

Above: Mark Philippoussis, well supported by a contingent of fellow countrymen, was too strong for Henman (opposite).

It was 8.23 p.m. on the Centre Court clock when Philippoussis delivered the second-serve, 34th ace which completed another amazing victory in five sets for the 23-year-old Australian. Henman, who had courageously and often brilliantly survived his opponent's breathtaking start well enough to inspire the belief that his Wimbledon crusade would continue, had simply been blown away by awesome serving power.

Devastated, Henman slammed his racket on the sole of his left foot and it crumpled, just like his aspirations. 'I gave it everything I had but he wore me down with his serve and as frustrated as I am I have to take my hat off to him and say he was too good today' said the British number one.

Henman gave everything he had and the way he turned things round after a 21-minute opening set in which he won only six points — just two off the Philippoussis serve which were both double faults — had the crowd round the court, and many more packed tightly on the viewing lawn following the action on the big screen, roaring their encouragement and approval.

Perhaps had Henman been able to take the last break point he was offered in the opening game of the fourth set, it might have been different. Philippoussis, though, saved it typically enough with a service winner in a game during which he also hit four aces.

The decisive break instead went to the 6ft 4in tenth seed in the seventh game of the final set when although Henman saved two break points from 0–40, he misjudged a mishit backhand lob on the third which, cruelly for him, landed on the baseline.

Henman had gone to 0–40 when he mishit a high backhand volley just as someone in the crowd delivered a celebratory shout thinking the point was about to be won. 'No excuses' Henman said. 'I should have made that shot. Unfortunately I missed it. I executed a lot of good shots but not that one.'

So after three hours 12 minutes, and

Keeping the best for last on the Order of Play became something of a pattern during Wimbledon 2000, even though it was more by chance than design. That was certainly the case on Day Seven when a double barrage of brilliant serving and returning ended Tim Henman and his supporters' dream that the new millennium might begin with the first British men's singles champion for 64 years.

*'Whether I win here or not, only time
will tell. I just want to be able to look
back at the end of my career and say
"I did everything I could. I worked as
hard as possible at all times." If it
happens, great. If it doesn't, I can't
have any complaints.'*

Tim Henman after losing to Mark
Philippoussis in the fourth round.

Joy for Byron Black (below) as he moved into the last eight but it was the end of the Wimbledon road this year for Wayne Ferreira (bottom left) — the latest victim of qualifier Vladimir Voltchkov — and David Prinosil (bottom right).

only 48 hours after he had spent five hours on court winning his previous round, Philippoussis won 6–1, 5–7, 6–7 (9–11), 6–3, 6–4, and demonstrated that his physical and mental stamina had never been greater.

Earlier Pete Sampras, showing few signs of his foot problem, had further impressed the Centre Court crowd as he served and often returned brilliantly to beat Jonas Bjorkman 6–3, 6–2, 7–5. Yet according to the defending champion, his popularity with the fans was not being matched among some of his fellow players. While carefully avoiding any direct accusations, Sampras said he was convinced some of them thought he was exaggerating the scale of his injury. 'I'm sure a lot of players think whatever they think. You can tell from comments you hear from here and there' he claimed. 'There are always going to be cynics in the world.'

'Is the foot all right now?' he was asked. 'OK, just OK' he replied, before adding 'I'm tired of talking about the injury. It is what it is. I'm going to go out there and try my best under the circumstance. I'm definitely going to give it everything I have. I'm sure there are a lot

of cynical players out there reading all this stuff. I could tell the way Jonas shook my hand today that he was thinking whatever he thinks.'

Bjorkman utterly rejected the suggestion and made it clear that, if there were players suspicious about the extent of the Sampras injury, he was not one of them and if there had been any lack of warmth in his handshake it was because he was disappointed to have lost after playing 'great tennis in the last two weeks'.

Sampras would next face Jan-Michael Gambill, who delivered another 33 aces as he added seventh-seeded Thomas Enqvist to his growing list of victims, with a 7–6, 3–6 6–3, 6–4 victory, while Andre Agassi advanced 6–4, 6–3, 6–3 against German qualifier, David Prinosil, and then pronounced 'This is the best I've felt in the tournament so far. Going into the quarters I feel I'm positioned now to play my best tennis.'

Pat Rafter, despite a lapse in the third set, the first he had lost in the tournament, beat the unseeded Thomas Johansson, who was also the last remaining Swede, 6–3, 6–4, 6–7, 6–1, while Alexander Popp continued his exciting exploits by dismissing the only opponent who could look him straight in the eye — fellow 6ft 7in player Marc Rosset — 6–1, 6–4, 3–6, 4–6, 6–1.

Yet the biggest surprise of the day was once more provided by 22-year-old qualifier, Vladimir Voltchkov, son of an electrician in a car plant in Minsk, who was having to beg or borrow extra tennis shoes to keep him going. Voltchkov looked increasingly composed and confident as he upset Richard Krajicek's conqueror, Wayne Ferreira, for a place in the last eight.

Ferreira, who had broken one racket in frustration earlier in the fortnight, looked as if he would like to have dealt similarly with another when he was left bewildered and frustrated as Voltchkov rounded off another superb display by taking the third set tie-break 7–0, finishing it with an ace for a stunning 6–3, 6–4, 7–6 triumph.

Pete Sampras's fine serving (far left) was vital again as he overcame Jonas Bjorkman (left) while Pat Rafter (below) was often at full stretch in resisting the challenge by Thomas Johansson.

Lindsay Davenport (right) benefited from a disappointing number of unforced errors from Jennifer Capriati as she reached the quarter finals together with, among others, the Williams sisters, Venus (far right) and Serena (below), who, more than anyone, was sweeping opponents aside with powerful ease.

Lisa Raymond (above right) emerged triumphant from her fourth round contest with Olga Barabanschikova (above left) who was also unseeded.

'We may only have synthetic grass courts at home but real grass is my best surface' said a beaming Voltchkov, who then turned his attention to playing Byron Black, a 4–6, 7–6, 6–2, 6–4 winner against Gianluca Pozzi.

In the ladies' singles, the eight winners who moved into the quarter finals all did so in straight sets and, in most cases, with a minimum of stress or excitement. Indeed the biggest flutter of the day when there were ladies on court came by a male streaker who did a forward roll over the net and then showed off the slogan on his chest which, as in Kournikova's brassière commercial, read 'Only the balls should bounce.' As the late cricket commentator, John Arlott said during a similar disruption at Lords, 'What a lot of fuss over such a little thing.'

Away from such nonsense most people were more looking forward to the ladies' quarter finals the next day than the matches which had just been played. The line-up which had been created was certainly appetising. Although Martina Hingis, who had brushed aside Anke

Huber 6–1, 6–2, was demonstrating a bold enough approach on the eve of a clash with Venus Williams the American too was starting to run into her most forceful form, even if she could not prevent the plucky Sabine Appelmans of Belgium saving 11 break points in one game before losing 6–4, 6–4.

Serena Williams brushed aside Tamarine Tanasugarn 6–1, 6–1 in 54 minutes in readiness for her next step against unseeded fellow American, Lisa Raymond; Jelena Dokic, highly impressive in a 6–1, 6–3 defeat of another American, Kristina Brandi, would next face Magui Serna of Spain, while lastly, another Lindsay Davenport–Monica Seles clash was in prospect.

Seles, as had been the case 18 times in the past, maintained the baseline barrage, with a few taunting drop shots in between, just a little more effectively as she beat Arantxa Sanchez-Vicario and Davenport advanced 6–3, 6–3 against Jennifer Capriati, who played rather more impressively than the score might suggest but still failed to sustain the challenge in the way she had hoped.

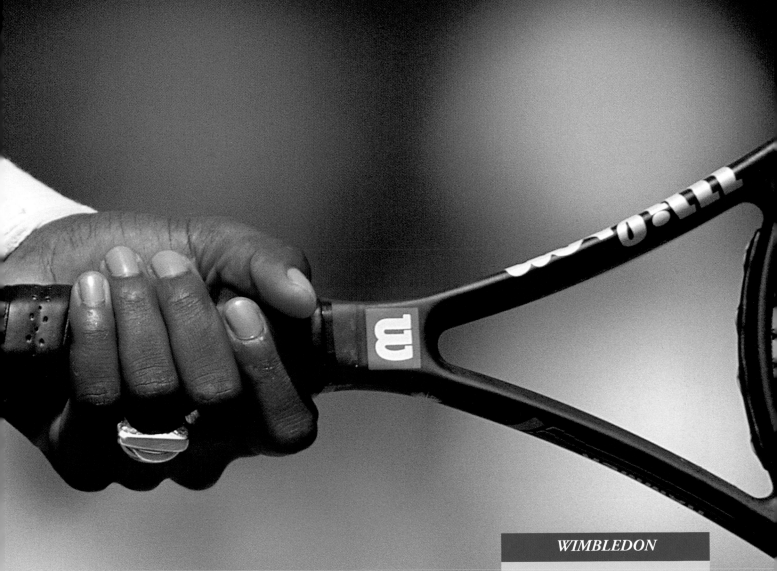

Another piece of Wimbledon history was made on Day Eight when Venus and Serena Williams surged to victory in their quarter finals to set up what would be only the third meeting between sisters at The Championships — and the first since the game went Open in 1968.

Not that there was likely to be much comparison between the two Americans, who were also partnering one another in doubles, and the initial encounter between siblings in the very first Wimbledon ladies' singles final in 1884. Maud v. Lilian Watson wore petticoats and corsets and served underarm.

Venus and Serena are leaders in tennis fashion, as well as being world class players, as their figure hugging dresses underlined. Venus, just 20, kept going for ferocious winners until enough had been struck to beat top-seeded former champion, Martina Hingis and Serena, still

18, ruthlessly dismissed fellow American, Lisa Raymond, in 42 minutes.

'The power and the glory' was how Sue Mott, of *The Daily Telegraph*, summed up their performances, after they had 'both played like furies' to celebrate, as good Americans, the Fourth of July.

The Centre Court crowd was enthralled by the breathless rallies and above all the scorching backhand crosscourt winners unleashed by Venus Williams as she moved to a 6–3, 4–6, 6–4 victory against an opponent who was tactically more astute but ultimately had to yield to the pace and ferocity of the American's hitting.

Williams was quickly into her stride, pouncing on her prey at every opportunity as she continued to keep Hingis on the back foot and, having broken serve a second time to lead 5–3 when the top seed played an unexpectedly loose

Martina Hingis (below) ultimately had to yield to the added power and tenacity of Venus Williams, who had put the pre-match advice from her father, Richard (opposite), to good use in the finest ladies' singles match of this year's Championships.

There was double joy for the Williams family when Serena (opposite) trounced Lisa Raymond (below) to ensure an historic semi-final meeting 48 hours later against her older sister.

eighth game, she delivered a booming ace to complete the first set.

Many of the rallies were long and exhausting, one of them spanning 22 strokes. Hingis broke for 5–3 in the second set after the most spectacular point of a memorable match. Williams raced back to reach a lob but slipped and she was sitting on the floor as Hingis put away the winner. The tension mounted.

Williams broke straight back but in her excitement became impetuous and despite saving four set points, was pushed into a deciding set.

Hingis's toilet break extended to seven minutes between the second and third sets, which began with no less than five consecutive breaks of serve before Williams held for 4–2. Despite a warning for a time violation, though, Hingis then

served out to love at 5–4. As her match-winning ace thundered into the back canvas, Venus leapt in the air and began cavorting joyously all round the court, while her father contented himself with a jog in the aisle alongside the players' box.

By contrast with this thriller which had ebbed and flowed on Centre Court, Serena looked totally dominant as she dismissed Lisa Raymond on No. 1 Court 6–2, 6–0. Serena broke to love in the first game, did so again for 4–1 and stormed on to a 6–2, 6–0 victory. The second set was a formality as Raymond simply fell apart under such a battering.

The Williams sisters both tried to suggest that their meeting two days hence would be 'just another match', though no-one really believed them. Their proud father, a devout Jehovah's Witness, said 'I think I'm going to have my first drink since 1958. I've no idea which of them will win but at least there's bound to be a Williams in the final.'

While still not functioning on full power, or with absolute conviction, Lindsay Davenport felt she was still making strides towards her best form, especially after she picked up the pace in the final set of her 6–7, 6–4, 6–0 defeat of Monica Seles. For a set and a half Davenport had been forced into an uncomfortable number of errors by piston-like groundstrokes driven deep into the corners by Seles but things changed after a mammoth sixth game of the second set.

'Certainly it wasn't the same in the third set as it had been for me in the first and second' said Seles, who from 3–3, when she saved nine break points in a game of ten deuces, never again held serve. After the drama of the Williams– Hingis match which had gone before, it was not a match which stirred the emotions.

While the quality of groundstrokes was impressive there was a disappointing lack of variety and shortage of real bite. Davenport admitted that once again it had largely been a case of her hanging in 'while my game got better and better. I'm just so happy I held my nerve and stayed focused' she said, although the

Below: Lindsay Davenport prepares to whack another of her winning forehands in her quarter final victory over Monica Seles.

easy forehand she missed with the court wide open at 5–3, 30–30 in the second set was further testimony to her shortage of matchplay.

Seles then gave herself another lifeline by breaking first with a softening up forehand to her opponent's backhand corner and then a winning backhand to the opposite corner. Even so she scorned this hard-won opportunity with a really weak tenth game in which Davenport then squandered two set points before clinching the third on a net cord. It was that kind of erratic match.

In her semi-final, Davenport would be facing Jelena Dokic for the first time. In beating Spain's Magui Serna, Dokic demonstrated that she can create rather more meaningful news than her explosively temperamental father, Damir, whose most recent curious act had been to sack Tony Roche as his daughter's coach.

Dokic's comfortable, though sometimes laboured 6–3, 6–2 win meant that she and Serena Williams were the only players left in either the men's or ladies' singles without dropping a set. Erasing any unhappy memories which might have been there from her defeat by Alexandra Stevenson in the same round a year earlier, Dokic quickly establishing a 3–0 lead in the first set and, despite spells when her tennis was riddled with errors, she always looked stronger on the points which seemed to matter — and that made the difference.

By now the doubles events were also approaching a significant stage and once again there was a large crowd to see the irrepressible Martina Navratilova and Mariaan de Swardt trounce Amélie Mauresmo and Arantxa Sanchez-Vicario, 6–1, 6–1 in readiness for a quarter final tilt at the Williams sisters.

The juniors were also in full swing and there was encouragement in the British camp as five home players, three girls and two boys, reached the third round of their respective events. Surrey's eighth-seeded Hannah Collin even achieved the distinction of beating the American, Ashley Harkleroad 6–3, 6–0 in 40 minutes. Scotland's Elena Baltacha and Anne Keothavong from Hackney joined her in the last 16, while in the boys there were victories for Somerset's Lee Childs, 3–6, 6–3, 9–7 over Hamid Mirzadeh from the United States and Matthew Smith, who won an all-British encounter against Chris Lewis, 6–0, 6–1.

Henri Leconte (far left), the ever-questioning Ilie Nastase (left) and an expansive John Newcombe (below) demonstrate that the competitive instincts live on among the seniors.

WIMBLEDON

day 9

WEDNESDAY 5 JULY

Andre Agassi was in his most explosive form, as illustrated opposite, as he outwitted Mark Philippoussis (below, with Agassi) in a splendid quarter final on the Centre Court.

In a sense one could say that normal service was resumed at Wimbledon for the quarter finals of the men's singles, as defending champion, Pete Sampras, former champion, Andre Agassi, and one who if fit would always be regarded as a potential champion, Pat Rafter, stayed on course for the final, with varying degrees of difficulty. Also progressing with them was one rank outsider — 237-ranked qualifier, Vladimir Voltchkov, who ended unseeded Byron Black's best year, 7–6, 7–6, 6–4.

There was no doubting the most im-

five-setters in previous rounds started to take their toll on Philippoussis, who came into the match with 132 aces already against his name during the fortnight and saw the figure edge its way past 150. Yet the main reason for the outcome was that Agassi chose this day to remind everyone in general and Philippoussis in particular why he is regarded as one of the best returners of serves in the game and why this asset is especially significant on grass.

Although Philippoussis won his opening service game to love, Agassi's determination either to take it on with a swinging return or wait his chance to pounce with a challenging response to any second serve, was clear, though, from the start and once he had taken the first set the mental battle had been won.

The crucial moment came with Agassi leading 4–3 in the tie-break. Philippoussis flung down a serve at 135 mph. Agassi smacked it straight back as if he was swatting an irritant fly and rounded off things 7–4 after 50 minutes, with an ace. In the second set the pattern was much the same with Agassi maintaining the pressure but waiting for the right moment to strike, except that this time there was no need for him to do so. Philippoussis double-faulted twice in the eighth game and allowed Agassi to serve out for it, 6–3.

Agassi strutted on confidently before offering his customary bows and kisses to all sides of the court. 'He has a fantastic serve' said Agassi 'one of the best in the game. But I don't get distracted by people acing me. I just try to make sure that I make the most of the opportunities which I know will eventually come my way. There's a lot which goes on out there which can allow you to get around one guy's particular weapon.'

Next up for Agassi would be Rafter, who would probably have liked a rather sharper test than was offered by Alexander Popp. The lofty German, playing at Wimbledon for the first time, suddenly appeared nervous at finding himself among the last eight and with Rafter

pressive performance on a day which began with many wondering if they would see any tennis at all if the weather predictions were fulfilled, let alone an almost full programme. It came from Agassi, who produced his most consistently effective form since winning The Australian Open in January to stunt the impact of that thunderous Mark Philippoussis serve which was too much for Tim Henman, 7–6, 6–3, 6–4.

Doubtless the physical effort of two

Another smooth passage for Pat Rafter (left) although Alexander Popp (below), towelling down at changeovers while pushing the Australian to a third set tie-break, had every reason to feel delighted by his success in reaching the last eight at his first Wimbledon.

hardly making an unforced error, it was all plain sailing for the Australian, who won 6–3, 6–2, 7–6.

Sampras never looked in serious danger against a courageous but luckless Jan-Michael Gambill, despite losing a set in his 6–4, 6–7, 6–4, 6–4 victory but it was not a particularly stirring performance either. Sampras waved to the crowd as he walked off court, pausing to sign a few autographs but the furrowed brow indicated his belief that the next four days could still be desperately difficult before a seventh title in eight years could be secured.

'If this was any other tournament I wouldn't play' admitted Sampras, with reference to the state of his injured left foot. 'I've been dealt this blow and there's not much I can do except do my best to work this out.' He said he was still unable to practice between matches and was 'trying everything' to help heal the problem, including acupuncture.

Gambill produced as many of the best moments of the match as Sampras. Yet his opponent's added experience was probably the key on such a difficult day mentally and physically for him. Under the pressure of having to hold his serve to stay in the first set, Gambill overhit the sort of backhand he had been putting away with ease to 30–40 and then double-faulted.

Gambill deservedly levelled in the second set tie-break but the third was decided by as fine a point as one is likely to see anywhere at any time. Gambill played a fine reaching backhand return off the serve by Sampras, who then drove a backhand deeply down the line. Gambill responded in kind, forcing a lunging backhand volley by Sampras which was worthy of being a winner. Gambill, though, not only reached it to strike another splendid shot of his own down the line but somehow managed to race back into mid-court to meet his opponent's next offering. This time Gambill's shot landed just over the baseline.

The player who, Sampras said, could have a big future kept fighting but he

was broken again in the ninth game of the fourth set and a relieved Sampras then served out for a place in the semi-finals with his 26th ace.

In booking a date with Sampras, Voltchkov emulated John McEnroe's 1977 performance of reaching the penultimate round of the tournament as a qualifier and, after beating Black in straight sets, he revealed the problems he

Pete Sampras (opposite) knew there was still a long way to go to reach peak form after taking four sets to subdue fellow American Jan-Michael Gambill (below), who produced some of the best moments of the match.

Above: The fairy-tale progress by qualifier Vladimir Voltchkov continued at the expense of Byron Black.

had endured off, rather than on, the court. He was wearing Nike shorts which were a gift from Marat Safin, an Adidas shirt and shoes by courtesy of both manufacturers. He also revealed that had he lost in the first round he would have been forced, for financial reasons, to return to Minsk before the Bristol Challenger instead of staying ten days in London at his own expense.

His latest victory was a roller-coaster ride for his growing army of supporters for he dropped his serve twice in every set but somehow managed to retrieve the situation each time before it was too late. The speed of his serves varied as much as the rest of his game. He saved a set point against him with an impudent delivery timed at 70 mph. Another break point was saved with a blockbuster almost twice that speed. As Black said 'At times I thought I had him but he kept coming up with big shots.'

Meanwhile on Court Two, Martina Navratilova's comeback in the doubles at the age of 43 came to an end when she and Mariaan de Swardt, who had lived dangerously in at least one earlier round, were beaten 4–6, 6–2, 6–1 by the Williams sisters, Venus and Serena. It was a fascinating contest with Navratilova dominating the scene like a headmistress for the first set before her opponents, like cheeky teenagers, realised that their heavier hitting — especially Serena's overheads — would have the decisive word.

Todd Woodbridge and Mark Woodforde, top seeds in the men's doubles, had a scare when from a set up they trailed two sets to one against Daniel Nestor and Sebastien Lareau of Canada. It was a tricky day too for second seeds Paul Haarhuis and Sandon Stolle before they overcame a two sets deficit against Roger Federer and Andrew Kratzmann, 6–7, 5–7, 7–6, 6–2, 6–2.

Britain's last remaining representatives in the junior singles were all beaten although Anne Keothavong took the first set from Hungary's fifth-seeded Aniko Kapros before being hustled to a 4–6, 6–1, 6–2 defeat. Hannah Collin, impressive the day before, was ruthlessly outplayed 6–1, 6–1 by Claudine Schaul of Luxemburg. Lee Childs took a set from Belgium's Kristof Vliegen but neither he nor Matthew Smith were able to reach the last eight.

Right: Mariaan de Swardt can't believe it and Martina Navratilova hides behind her racket in embarrassment as a shot off the frame becomes a fluke winner during the ladies' doubles. Navratilova, though, showed she could still produce athletically classic shots (below).

Overleaf: Perfect concentration at the net by Venus Williams as Serena serves on their way towards the ladies' doubles final.

'I thought I was big but I'm a pip-squeak next to them.'

Martina Navratilova talking about the Williams sisters.

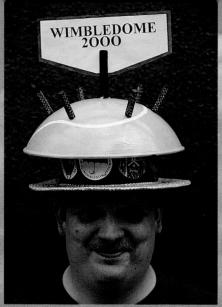

WIMBLEDOME 2000

THE CHAMPIONSHIPS

On the eve of only the third meeting between sisters in the history of The Championships, three times former champion Chris Evert said it would be 'a difficult match for all concerned — the players and the spectators.' Despite the power play which flowed from both sides of the court for most of the 87 minutes neither Venus nor Serena played to their full potential while it was not until well into the second set — and then only occasionally — that the crowd demonstrated more than respectful appreciation.

The prolonged moment of shocked silence after Serena double-faulted on match point, before the crowd rose to offer a standing ovation, seemed to sum up their understanding of the stresses the sisters must have been experiencing.

It was almost as if they had not wanted to take sides in such a sporting family contest. Just as an older sister tends to prevail in most contests, sporting or otherwise, so Venus ultimately emerged the victor, 6–2, 7–6, principally because her serve was the more potent on the day. Serena also probably suffered from not having been seriously challenged in any of her previous five matches in which she had conceded only 13 games in ten sets, whereas Venus's confidence was sky high after beating Martina Hingis in such a high-pressure match one round earlier.

Through no fault of her own, Serena, who in normal circumstances would have constantly been trying to get to the net first and take the initiative, had never needed to improvise in earlier matches. That made it all the more difficult for her to do so once her forehand went walkabout as she lost the service break she had been holding until the oh-so-vital seventh game of the second set.

Both in a mediocre first set and again when Venus was taking 11 consecutive points as she recovered from 2–4 to lead 5–4 in the second, Serena needed to try something different. To do that, however, against someone with whom she had not only practised that morning but

all her life and who had been taught to play in exactly the same way, was asking too much.

Serena paid a heavy price for missing too many of the big points. The statistics were revealing. While she struck more than twice the number of winners as her older sister — 24 compared with 11 — she also hit 43 unforced errors, 18 more than Venus.

For a moment tears were not far away after Serena double-faulted on match point and Venus sensitively made no attempt to demonstrate any celebratory feelings. Instead she wrapped a comforting arm around the little sister she had so often looked after in previous significant times in their lives and said 'Let's get outta here.'

There was no shortage of cynics who questioned whether the match had been for real or whether, because Serena had already won a Grand Slam title at the US Open nine months earlier, there had been a family conference which decreed it would now be Venus's turn. Both girls refuted the suggestion and certainly Serena's abject misery in the moment of defeat seemed to be ample evidence that this was true.

While events in the past, when the girls' father, Richard Williams, intimated that he might not allow both his daughters to compete in the same tournaments, may have contributed to some of the doubts being held, Lindsay Davenport put the issue into context when she was asked if the outcome had been fixed.

'No, I don't think that at all' she said firmly. 'If you watched, it seemed like they were trying. Mentally I think it might have been tougher for the younger one. That also goes for things outside tennis.'

As for her own semi-final, Davenport beat Jelena Dokic, the 17-year-old Australian, in another match which failed to live up to expectations. With both players making a disappointing array of unforced errors, it never took off and both seemed apologetic.

'Obviously I didn't play so well as I

The power Venus Williams puts into her serve is illustrated (opposite) by the way the ball becomes flattened against the strings of the racket on impact.

Below: The sisters pose before their historic semi-final meeting.

It was a difficult day for them both but Serena sportingly manages a smile in defeat.

A splendid double-handed backhand from Jelena Dokic (below) but there were not quite enough of them from the teenager as a naturally happy Lindsay Davenport (opposite) once more took her place in the final.

could and wanted to' said Dokic who, despite some early impressive backhand winners, was unable to cope with Davenport's heavier weight of shot. The Californian second seed effectively acknowledged the modest quality of a

match in which there were seven service breaks in ten games in the first set when she said 'When you have two players who aren't necessarily playing their best, you just play as well as you need to win. That was the case on this occasion.

'I would love to have served better in the first set and maybe, being her first Grand Slam semi-final, it was a bit over-whelming for her. It was too bad that neither of us played a bit better.'

Elsewhere Todd Woodbridge and Mark Woodforde continued their efforts to regain the men's doubles title they last won in 1997 when, without reaching their imposing best, they reached the final with a 6–4, 7–6, 6–2 defeat of Sweden's Nicklas Kulti and Mikael Tillstrom. Their opponents for the title were to be Holland's Paul Haarhuis and Sandon Stolle, who were pushed rather harder for their 6–4, 7–6, 6–7, 6–4 victory over the South Africans, David Adams and John-Laffnie De Jager.

The pace was also picking up in the mixed doubles, where several names of stalwart doubles players were evident in third round victories, including veteran American, Rick Leach, partnered by Amanda Coetzer although later in the day they went out 6–1, 7–6 to Joshua Eagle and Anke Huber. There were also teenagers making their mark, among them Australia's Lleyton Hewitt and Belgium's Kim Clijsters, who came from a set down to win a second-set tie-break 10–8 on their way to beating Eric Taino and Katie Schlukebir of the United States for a place in the semi-finals.

On the outside courts one of the largest crowds packed round Court 14 to savour the familiar but always amusing clowning antics of Mansour Bahrami and Henri Leconte in the 35-and-over doubles round-robin event. The rules of tennis are often bent to allow full impact for the jokes and trick shots when the French pair are around. The crowd lapped it up and happily John Lloyd and Christo Van Rensburg, who were beaten 6–3, 6–4, took it in the spirit in which it was intended.

WIMBLEDON

day 11

FRIDAY 7 JULY

Pat Rafter's joy (below) is evident, after his brilliant backhand returns, illustrated in the previous spread, had been the key as he wore down former champion Andre Agassi (opposite) in five sets to reach his first Wimbledon final.

This was a day when one Wimbledon dream suddenly became a real possibility and another, which had survived, with increasing excitement through eight matches, came to a noble end.

Less than four months after Pat Rafter felt so frustrated by his slow recovery from surgery on his right shoulder that he was not even sure he would compete at The Championships, let alone thrive there, the popular Aus-

tralian took revenge for defeat by the same opponent at the same stage a year earlier, by winning a thrilling semi-final against Andre Agassi.

Victory not only gave him a great chance of adding the Wimbledon crown to the two successive US Open trophies he collected in 1997–98 but also the opportunity to earn extended joint ownership, for fellow Australian Roy Emerson, of the Grand Slam record of winning 12 men's singles titles.

With Rafter safely through to the final, Pete Sampras, the American still one elusive success away from being out on his own with a 13th title, followed him on to Centre Court to bring the

curtain down on the emotional rags-to-riches journey which Belarusian, Vladimir Voltchkov, had been making since stepping on to the courts in Roehampton in the first of his three qualifying tournament matches.

It was during the ATP Tour Masters Series event at Key Biscayne in March that Rafter's confidence and motivation seemed to be sinking to their lowest level, as the shoulder continued to restrict his serve — and therefore significantly diminish the effectiveness of his whole game.

Even going into the French Open, a month before Wimbledon, his comments and body language remained such that urgent morale-boosting efforts by his Davis Cup captain, John Newcombe and coach, Tony Roche, were appropriate. Roche, a former singles runner-up at Wimbledon and five times a doubles champion, was in the players' box, clearly content as Rafter, always more aggressive and bolder on more of the biggest points, completed his 7–5, 4–6, 7–5, 4–6, 6–3 success in three hours 18 minutes.

Much of the tennis was of the highest quality — the best to date in the men's singles during the tournament. It was one of the most consistently competitive and gripping semi-finals since that classic in 1977 when Bjorn Borg beat Vitas Gerulaitis.

Then, though, there was barely a handful of unforced errors from either man. This time there were infinitely more wonderful winners than extravagant mistakes although in each of the three sets Agassi lost he double-faulted at the worst possible times.

Trailing 6–5 in the opening set, Agassi, who had been denied the sole break point of the set by a Rafter serve in the fifth game, double-faulted to 30–40 and his opponent pounced gleefully to take the initiative. Having broken twice to level in the second set and also broken back the first time Rafter served for the third set, Agassi played his poorest game of the day.

Whereas Rafter had been dominating

Hard though Vladimir Voltchkov (opposite) chased and challenged, there was nothing he could do to prevent Pete Sampras (below) taking his customary place in the final.

at the net, Agassi had been equally effective with his passes but then two double faults undermined much of the fine work the American had put in earlier in that set and Rafter, who looked just as adept at going for quick winners as he was in waiting for the right moment in longer rallies, broke with a great forehand cross-court winner.

When Agassi saved five break-back points in the second game of the fourth set, which included seven deuces, he believed the match was starting to turn his way but Rafter stayed firm, never lost his serve again and then had the encouragement of serving first in the fifth — just as he had done in the previous four.

'I think that told against me' said Agassi. 'It might have been different if I'd been serving first in the fifth.' Increasingly one felt that the first break would be decisive. So it was, although it was with the help of another Agassi double fault which left him 30–40. There was no way back. Agassi netted a forehand on his second attempt at thwarting Rafter covering the net and Rafter then served out twice to deserve his passport into the final.

Sampras was clearly still struggling with the inflamed ligaments in his left ankle, so much so that he twice called for trainer Doug Spreen to apply a cooling ointment on them, but once he had taken the opening set tie-break, by courtesy of a missed backhand volley from Voltchkov when he was 3–4, it was over as a meaningful contest.

The top seed won 7–6, 6–2, 6–4 but it was still a heart-warming occasion for Voltchkov, as the knowledgeable Centre Court crowd left him in no doubt that they appreciated not just the many fine serves and exploding forehands he had treated them to during the match but also his memorable progress through first the qualifying and then the main draw.

While Voltchkov wondered if, apart from prize money of £119,380, almost three times his on-court earnings in the previous year, any sponsorship deals would be forthcoming, Sampras still had to worry about getting himself fit for the final. 'It's still sore and it's definitely been a struggle but I'm still here and so long as I have my right arm, I always think I have a chance here at Wimbledon.'

After being on opposite sides of the net a day earlier, Venus and Serena were

back in perfect harmony as they moved into the final of the ladies' doubles with a rousing performance to upset the higher-seeded Anna Kournikova and Natasha Zvereva, 6–3, 7–6. Serena Williams, who hit the clinching smash on their fourth match point had a beaming smile, after that heartbroken frown at the end of her singles but said it was not really full consolation. Zvereva was not happy. A gesture she made reflecting frustration at the end led to her being fined.

There was also a seeding upset in the other semi-final when top seeds Lisa Raymond and Rennae Stubbs, favourites after the withdrawal of defending champions Lindsay Davenport and

Corina Morariu, following Morariu's opening day singles injury, were beaten in three sets. They looked to be in control when leading 3–0 in the first set but once the fluctuating second was won by Julie Halard-Decugis and Ai Sugiyama, the momentum changed and they were beaten 3–6, 7–5, 6–2.

In the mixed doubles, the performance of the day came from Lleyton Hewitt and his Belgian girl friend, Kim Clijsters, as they carved out a tight 6–4, 7–5 victory over his Australian team-mate, Joshua Eagle and Germany's Anke Huber. It set up the possibility of a third major title going to Australia in tandem with Rafter in the singles and the amazing 'Woodies' in the men's doubles.

Anna Kournikova, serving, and Natasha Zvereva (opposite) had high hopes of reaching the ladies' doubles final — until they found the Williams sisters (below) just too good for them tactically and physically.

'It's impossible to beat the two of us.'
Venus Williams after she and Serena reached the final of the ladies' doubles.

The headlines said it all. 'Venus in Orbit' cried several of the newspapers on the morning after Venus Williams, wearing an orange-trimmed, backless white dress became the first black player to carry off the ladies' singles trophy since Althea Gibson in 1958. And just as Gibson's awesome supremacy, which also enabled her successfully to defend the title one year later, was based on wonderful athleticism, as well as all-round skills and court craft, so Venus's speed about the court, allied to her famous power proved too much for defending champion, Lindsay Davenport, whose game never really took off.

For many the one regret as they watched the worthy new champion climb her way through the stand to accept congratulations from family and friends, while her father Richard danced precariously on the roof of a commentary box where Chris Evert was trying to describe the scene to American television viewers, was that Gibson was not present at the occasion.

Not well enough to travel from her home in New Jersey, either for the champions' parade a week earlier or for the final, Gibson had relayed a good-luck message to Venus through their mutual friend, Zina Garrison, although it was not conveyed until after she had become champion — 'in case it made her more nervous' Garrison explained. The message was still greatly appreciated. 'It's a privilege for me to win this while Althea is still alive' said Venus.

This first ladies' singles final between two American-born players since Billie-Jean King beat Chris Evert in her first final in 1973 was not a classic. Williams's supremacy, once she had overcome the loss of her serve in the first game and raced to a 4–1 lead in the opening set, was always too evident for real drama to unfold. Nor did a 30-minute delay after one false start, while everyone waited for another bout of that infuriating light drizzle to pass, help. Yet it was always a fascinating contest, not least when Davenport was more than

once offered a way back while her opponent suddenly wobbled when serving for a 5–3 lead in the second set.

Basically though, Davenport could not cope whenever Williams was in full flow. She was frequently to be found dashing and lunging to make a return

Previous spread: Sue Barker interviews Venus Williams after the match.

The magic moment of triumph for Venus Williams (opposite), as Lindsay Davenport (below) realises her proud year as the reigning ladies' champion is over.

Below: Venus Williams clambers through the crowd to meet family and friends, as father Richard stands on the commentary box roof.

on one flank before having to charge to the other, hoping to do exactly the same. It took its toll. Not that Davenport did not give everything she had to try and keep the title which meant so much to her.

She saved one set point at 5–2 in the second set and another one game later before overhitting a forehand on the third. Davenport then moved into a 2–0 lead in the second set but suddenly Williams revealed not just power but also a fine touch with a brilliant backhand drop shot from mid-court which helped her break back. And despite three double faults which left Williams a break down for a second time, Davenport was again unable to take her chance and once more fell behind.

The tense, topsy-turvy nature of the set continued as Davenport broke back to 4–4 with one of her finest forehand

volleys but if that was the shot of a champion determined to retain her status, what happened in the following was most certainly not. Under pressure at 15–40 after a double fault and a ferocious forehand on the 14th stroke of a pulsating rally, she completely mis-timed her backhand which flew long and gave Williams the opening to serve out for the match.

This time Williams fluffed it, making four unforced errors, two of them double faults. Once again Davenport's added experience could have taken charge but despite playing some of her best tennis of the afternoon to take it to a tie-break she went from 1–0 to 1–5 and could never recover.

Williams was a worthy champion and what made her achievement all the more remarkable was that the final was only her 16th match of the year — less than

Left: HRH The Duke of Kent, President of the All England Club, and Tim Phillips offer their congratulations as Venus Williams and Lindsay Davenport show their trophies to the world's media (below) before Venus takes her lap of honour (overleaf).

Mark Woodforde puts away another winner as Todd Woodbridge watches intently (above) as they impose their authority on Paul Haarhuis and Sandon Stolle (right) in the final of the men's doubles.

any other Wimbledon champion in Open tennis history. Asked to use one word to describe her feelings, Williams replied 'Proud.' Quite right too.

Davenport said 'I was hoping for a little more out of myself' although it was increasingly evident from early in the second set that she was struggling to overcome the problems with her leg and back which had also robbed her of so much pre-Wimbledon matchplay and restricted her mobility. 'Considering the circumstances, getting to the final was one of the toughest things I've done in my career' she said.

There was more emotion to follow on Centre Court. Mark Woodforde, who had already announced that he would be packing away his racket at the end of the year and Todd Woodbridge, who plans to continue with a new partner, registered a modern record sixth Wimbledon title and a record 60th on the men's Tour when they beat fellow Australian, Sandon Stolle and Paul Haarhuis of Holland 6–3, 6–4, 6–1.

Woodforde, 34, the senior member of the partnership by five years, said he wanted to experience some 'normality' before he was too old to enjoy it. Also he and his wife, Erin, were expecting their first child in January, a few weeks after Woodbridge's and his wife Natasha's baby would be due.

The on-court harmony of the champions could be uncanny. Just one break, when Stolle lost his serve in the sixth game, settled the first set, which was interrupted by rain when the eventual winners were leading 5–2. In the second set Haarhuis was broken in the seventh game and twice in the fourth as the 'Woodies', as they are affectionately known, went on to their triumph.

The point which took them to match point could stand as their monument. Woodforde's craft and guile prompted him to loop up a curving, tantalising lob. Woodbridge, perfectly placed, volleyed away their opponent's defensive response.

As they were presented with their

trophy in the Royal Box, it was almost as if they were reluctant to leave, especially Woodforde. The partners, who together had won around £10.5 million received a standing ovation from a packed crowd on the court where they had reigned supreme so often and in such style. 'This was perfect' said Woodbridge. 'I was very pleased that today, win or lose, we were going to end our

'We've done it again!' Todd Woodbridge (below, left) and Mark Woodforde go to hug each other after becoming Wimbledon champions for a modern record sixth time.

Top-seeded Frenchman, Nicolas Mahut (left) on his way to victory in the final of the boys' singles against Croatia's Mario Ancic (below) while (opposite) Argentina's Maria Salerni (top), the previous year's doubles champion, upset the higher-ranked Tatiana Perebiynis (below) of the Ukraine to win the girls' singles title.

partnership on Wimbledon's Centre Court. It was the perfect scenario.'

'Wimbledon is everything to us' added Woodforde. 'This is fabulous. They've always treated us with great care here.' He smiled and did not rule out the possibility, when asked if one day he and Woodbridge might resume their partnership in the 35-and-overs.

Meanwhile Donald Johnson and Kimberly Po reached the final of the mixed doubles with a 6–3, 6–4 victory over Nicolas Lapentti of Ecuador and Austria's Barbara Schett. Lapentti was to make much more of an impact on the same No. 1 Court a week later when, together with his 17-year-old brother, Giovanni, who had lost in the second round of the boys' singles at The Championships, he inspired a stunning Davis Cup World Group qualifying round victory over Britain — Ecuador's first Davis Cup win outside the Americas.

For the moment though there was still some British encouragement when Andrew Banks and Ben Riby upset the fourth seeds, Karol Beck of Slovakia and Michal Kokta of the Czech Republic, 7–6, 6–2 to become the first British finalists in the event since 1995 — Martin Lee, still struggling to establish himself on the ATP Tour, and James Trotman, now a coach in La Manga. Their success helped compensate for the disappointment when Somerset's burly Lee Childs and James Nelson from Northumberland, the top seeds, were beaten 1–6, 6–4, 6–3 by Dominic Coene and Kristof Vliegen of Belgium.

Nicolas Mahut of France justified his top seeding by taking the boys' singles title with a 3–6, 6–3, 7–5 victory over Croatian, Mario Ancic, while Argentina's Maria Emilia Salerni, seeded four, became the first Argentinian winner of a junior singles title at Wimbledon when she beat Tatiana Perebiynis of the Ukraine 6–4, 7–5. Salerni's hopes of a double triumph ended when in the doubles final, 48 hours later, she and Daja Bedanova of the Czech Republic, the holders, lost to Ioana Gaspar of Romania and Perebiynis, 7–6, 6–3.

days 13&14

SUNDAY 9 JULY & MONDAY 10 JULY

Right: Anthony Mills, 17 from Surrey, was nominated to toss the coin to decide whether Pete Sampras or Pat Rafter served first in the final. Anthony represented the Sargent Cancer Care for Children charity chosen by The Duchess of Kent and Tim Henman.

Opposite: Pete Sampras embraces his father, Sam, who was at Wimbledon for the first time as his son won a record 13th Grand Slam title.

Below: Detail of the Wimbledon 2000 flowerbed.

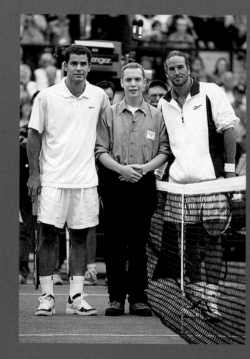

Opposite: Sampras won despite a bold bid by Pat Rafter (below) to ruin the American's party.

So to the men's singles final, which became another piece of true Wimbledon theatre, spread over three acts before reaching a tumultuous climax at 8.57 p.m. with Pete Sampras weeping on the Centre Court after becoming the game's most prolific winner of men's singles titles at Grand Slams.

Almost six hours after first walking onto his favourite arena and after two frustrating breaks in the opening set for

rain, Sampras, usually so reluctant to convey the most powerful emotions churning within him, was overcome as he completed his 6–7, 7–6, 6–4, 6–2 victory over a worthy finalist, Pat Rafter.

It was 3.02 p.m., just over an hour late, when the rain first allowed the final to get under way. Rafter had just edged into a 4–3 lead 26 minutes later after a seventh game of six deuces, when the Scotch mist which had returned meant the court had to be covered. It was a relatively brief delay of 26 minutes but there had only been time for Sampras, who was serving brilliantly, to hold for 4–4 and for Rafter to save the first three break points of the match in reaching a third deuce in the ninth game, before play was stopped again.

This time it quickly became evident that a lengthy disruption was inevitable. Indeed the rain was so heavy and so prolonged that many began to wonder if the match might have to be postponed until the following day. Suddenly, though, the clouds parted, even the sun appeared and at 6.34 p.m., in true Wimbledon style, with hardly an empty seat, this historic contest was under way once more.

Nowhere else in the world do tennis fans demonstrate the stoicism, determination and optimism so often shown by Wimbledon spectators frustrated by the weather. Seldom has their patience been more gloriously rewarded. They were to watch, first with considerable doubt but then with undiluted admiration and appreciation, as Sampras won his seventh title in eight years. That meant he had equalled William Renshaw's record of a seventh win in 1889, when the champion from one year only had to win one match 12 months later to keep the crown. It also earned the American his 13th Grand Slam title, one more than Roy Emerson.

What added to Sampras's delight as he played himself through the continuing pain of his foot injury, was that his parents, Sam and Georgia, had responded to his appeal to them, after he had won his semi-final, to fly from Los

Opposite: Pete Sampras holds the Wimbledon trophy aloft — a familiar sight but an even more special occasion this time — as his coach, Paul Annacone, left in the front row (below) and fiancée Bridgette Wilson, also savour the moment.

Angeles to watch him at Wimbledon for the first time. 'I've always wanted them to see me play here and it means so much to me that they are here' he said after following the now well-worn path of champions by climbing up into the stand to celebrate with them. 'I love Wimbledon, I love playing here. This is the best court in the world' he said.

Only once before had his parents watched him in a Grand Slam final. That had been at the US Open in 1992, when he was defending the title but lost it to Stefan Edberg. 'And I thought I was on my way to losing again here' he added, recalling how he had lost the first set and had trailed 4–1 in the tie-break in the second.

Rafter, who also missed key chances in the third set, said 'I had my opportunities early on but when you play a great champion like Pete, you have to take them. I got a bit nervous. I knew what was on the line but hopefully I'll be back next year and we'll see what happens.' Even so the day was still a memorable

one for the Australian who had more than justified the seeding committee's decision to recognise his obvious grass court ability, albeit at the expense of some offended clay court Spaniards.

Barely a month earlier he had still been struggling to recover from surgery on his right shoulder. 'I just wasn't expecting anything this year' he said. 'Anything that was going to happen would be a bonus — and even reaching the final here is a pretty big bonus.'

Sampras looked much the sharper for much of the first set but it turned firmly in Rafter's favour in the closing stages of a thrilling 22-point tie-break. Three times he snapped back from being a mini-break down and he saved the first of Sampras's two set points before his determination enabled him to take it 12–10. Sampras, who had saved the second of Rafter's set points with an ace, double-faulted to offer a third, which he also escaped, but then double-faulted yet again on the fourth.

The second set also went to a tie-break

Below: The Williams sisters at the Champions' Dinner.

without a service break. By then Rafter was the one playing with added assurance and when he led 4–1 he looked poised to establish a commanding advantage. Yet Sampras rescued one mini-break with a whipped forehand, was handed back the second on a double fault and Rafter then compounded that error by missing a forehand cross-court return which would have given him a 5–4 lead with two serves to follow.

Sampras's joy as he struck a brilliant forehand pass to earn two set points, was plain to see and he took the set on the second of them with a typically potent volley. From then on he steadily became the master. The third set turned in the fifth game when, having saved three break points, a tiring Rafter double-faulted and then netted a simple fore-hand volley.

The vital breakthrough in the fourth came when Sampras took a 3–2 lead when Rafter left a looping backhand on the third break point go, expecting it to fall out but it just dropped on the base-line behind him.

Peter Fleming and Sandy Mayer beat the Amritraj brothers, Vijay and Anand, 6–2, 6–4 in the men's 45-and-over invitation doubles while Ros Nideffer and Yvonne Vermaak beat Virginia Wade and Gretchen Magers 6–4, 6–2 in the final of the ladies' 35-and-over invitation doubles but the weather ruined some other best laid plans.

The final of the men's 35-and-over invitation doubles had to be divided between the British pair of Jeremy Bates and Nick Fulwood and the American holders, Ken Flach and Robert Seguso, while it also caused havoc for those organising The Champions' Dinner. Sampras, who did not finish media interviews until 11 p.m. only just made it in time with just a blazer over his tennis clothes, to respond to the toast to the champions just before Venus Williams made her speech and then had to leave with Serena to prepare for the ladies' doubles, held over until a 14th day.

Despite the short notice, long queues formed during the night and by the time the sisters went out to begin what became a comfortable 6–3, 6–2 defeat of Ai Sugiyama of Japan and Julie Halard-De-cugis, 9,159 were waiting to greet them on the Centre Court. Seldom has there been such an enthusiastic atmosphere for the ladies' doubles final and it was plain who most of the crowd were supporting — a pair of sisters who over the previous two weeks had created such excitement and won such admiration.

'We told you no-one could beat us' — the Williams sisters (left) show off the ladies' doubles trophy to the huge crowd (below), some of whom had queued overnight to watch the postponed final at lunchtime on the third Monday, watched by another 4.2 million on BBC Television alone.

The Ladies' Doubles Championship
Venus Williams & Serena Williams

The Mixed Doubles Championship
Kimberly Po & Donald Johnson

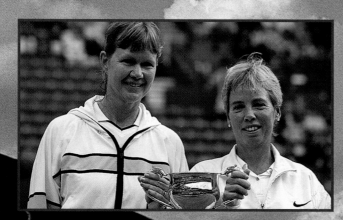

The 35 and over Ladies' Invitation Doubles
Rosalyn Nideffer & Yvonne Vermaak

The 35 and over Gentlemen's Invitation Doubles
Title shared: Ken Flach & Robert Seguso
and Jeremy Bates & Nick Fulwood
No presentation made

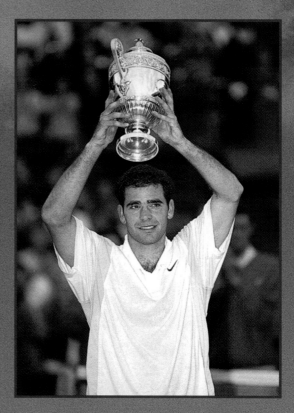

The Gentlemen's Singles Championship
Pete Sampras

The Boys' Doubles Championship
Dominique Coene & Kristof Vliegen

The Girls' Doubles Championship
Tatiana Perebiynis & Ioana Gaspar

The Ladies' Singles Championship
Venus Williams

The Gentlemen's Doubles Championship
Mark Woodforde & Todd Woodbridge

The Boys' Singles Championship
Nicolas Mahut

The Girls' Singles Championship
Maria Salerni

The 45 and over Gentlemen's Invitation Doubles
Peter Fleming & Sandy Mayer

CHAMPIONSHIP RECORDS

2000

ALPHABETICAL LIST OF COMPETITORS

LADIES

108 Ahl Miss L.A. *(Great Britain)*
19 Appelmans Miss S. *(Belgium)*
Arendt Miss N. *(USA)*
78 Arn Miss G. *(Germany)*
75 Asagoe Miss S. *(Japan)*
10 Bacheva Miss L. *(Bulgaria)*
Bachmann Miss A. *(Germany)*
47 Barabanschikova Miss O. *(Belarus)*
Barclay Miss C.G. *(Australia)*
61 Basting Miss Y. *(Netherlands)*
119 Basuki Miss Y. *(Indonesia)*
51 Bedanova Miss D. *(Czech Republic)*
Bes Miss E. *(Spain)*
25 Black Miss C. *(Zimbabwe)*
Bollegraf Miss M.M. *(Netherlands)*
18 Boogert Miss K. *(Netherlands)*
70 Brandi Miss K. *(USA)*
Buth Miss D. *(USA)*
99 Callens Miss E.S.H. *(Belgium)*
Canepa Miss A. *(Italy)*
114 Capriati Miss J. *(USA)*
63 Carlsson Miss A. *(Sweden)*
4 Casoni Miss G. *(Italy)*
6 Chladkova Miss D. *(Czech Republic)*
66 Clijsters Miss K. *(Belgium)*
89 Cocheteux Miss A. *(France)*
81 Coetzer Miss A.J. *(South Africa)*
12 Collin Miss H. *(Great Britain)*
67 Courtois Miss L. *(Belgium)*
102 Cristea Miss C. *(Romania)*
Crook Miss H. *(Great Britain)*
94 Cross Miss K.M. *(Great Britain)*
128 Davenport Miss L.A. *(USA)*
Davies Miss V.E. *(Great Britain)*
De Beer Miss S. *(South Africa)*
36 De Lone Miss E.R. *(USA)*
56 De Los Rios Miss R. *(Paraguay)*
73 de Swardt Miss M. *(South Africa)*
De Villiers Miss N. *(South Africa)*
27 Dechy Miss N. *(France)*
46 Dementieva Miss E. *(Russia)*
Dhenin Miss C. *(France)*
77 Dokic Miss J. *(Australia)*
20 Dragomir Miss R. *(Romania)*
9 Drake Miss M. *(Canada)*
Dyrberg Miss E. *(Denmark)*
Ellwood Miss A. *(Australia)*
84 Farina Miss S. *(Italy)*
41 Frazier Miss A. *(USA)*
Fusai Miss A. *(France)*
122 Gagliardi Miss E. *(Switzerland)*
124 Garbin Miss T. *(Italy)*
62 Gersi Miss A. *(Czech Republic)*
109 Grande Miss R. *(Italy)*
Grant Miss K. *(South Africa)*
60 Grzybowska Miss M. *(Poland)*
98 Habsudova Miss K. *(Slovak Republic)*
17 Halard-Decugis Mrs J. *(France)*
111 Henin Miss J. *(Belgium)*
1 Hingis Miss M. *(Switzerland)*
Hiraki Miss R. *(Japan)*
Hopkins Miss J. *(USA)*
59 Hopmans Miss A. *(Netherlands)*
Horn Miss L. *(South Africa)*
31 Hrdlickova Miss K. *(Czech Republic)*
16 Huber Miss A. *(Germany)*
Husarova Miss J. *(Slovak Republic)*
120 Irvin Miss M. *(USA)*
35 Jeyaseelan Miss S. *(Canada)*
21 Jidkova Miss A. *(Russia)*
38 Kandarr Miss J. *(Germany)*
43 Kleinova Miss S. *(Czech Republic)*
Kolbovic Miss R. *(Canada)*
105 Kostanic Miss J. *(Croatia)*
Koulikovskaya Miss E. *(Russia)*
50 Kournikova Miss A. *(Russia)*
91 Krasnoroutskaya Miss L. *(Russia)*
34 Kremer Miss A. *(Luxembourg)*
Kriventcheva Miss S. *(Bulgaria)*
Krizan Miss T. *(Slovenia)*
69 Kruger Miss J. *(South Africa)*
85 Kuti Kis Miss R. *(Hungary)*
72 Labat Miss F. *(Argentina)*
14 Latimer Miss L. *(Great Britain)*
79 Leon Garcia Miss G. *(Spain)*
125 Likhovtseva Miss E. *(Russia)*
Loit Miss E. *(France)*
5 Lucic Miss M. *(Croatia)*
90 Maleeva Miss M. *(Bulgaria)*
23 Mandula Miss P. *(Hungary)*
22 Marosi-Aracama Mrs K. *(Hungary)*
Martincova Miss E. *(Czech Republic)*
33 Martinez Miss C. *(Spain)*
80 Mauresmo Miss A. *(France)*
McNeil Miss L.M. *(USA)*
McQuillan Miss R. *(Australia)*
McShea Miss L. *(Australia)*
Miyagi Miss N. *(Japan)*
44 Molik Miss A. *(Australia)*
Montalvo Miss L. *(Argentina)*
2 Montolio Miss A. *(Spain)*
127 Morariu Miss C. *(USA)*
Musgrave Miss T. *(Australia)*
68 Myskina Miss A. *(Russia)*
106 Nacuk Miss S. *(Yugoslavia)*
37 Nagyova Miss H. *(Slovak Republic)*
Navratilova Miss M. *(USA)*
Neiland Mrs L. *(Latvia)*
39 Nejedly Miss J. *(Canada)*
57 Noorlander Miss S. *(Netherlands)*
92 Oremans Miss M. *(Netherlands)*
83 Osterloh Miss L. *(USA)*
71 Ostrovskaya Miss N. *(Belarus)*
103 Panova Miss T. *(Russia)*
13 Parkinson Miss H. *(USA)*
45 Petrova Miss N. *(Russia)*
96 Pierce Miss M. *(France)*
11 Pisnik Miss T. *(Slovenia)*
104 Pitkowski Miss S. *(France)*
117 Plischke Miss S. *(Austria)*
Po Miss K. *(USA)*
Poutchek Miss T. *(Belarus)*
95 Pratt Miss N.J. *(Australia)*
54 Pullin Miss J.M. *(Great Britain)*
Rampre Miss P. *(Slovenia)*
40 Raymond Miss L.M. *(USA)*
Reeves Miss S. *(USA)*
Riera Miss G. *(Spain)*
74 Rippner Miss B. *(USA)*
101 Rittner Miss B. *(Germany)*
Ruano Pascual Miss V. *(Spain)*
28 Rubin Miss C. *(USA)*
116 Sanchez Lorenzo Miss MA. *(Spain)*
112 Sanchez Vicario Miss A. *(Spain)*
48 Schett Miss B. *(Austria)*
Schlukebir Miss K. *(USA)*
110 Schnell Miss M. *(Austria)*
123 Schnyder Miss P. *(Switzerland)*
107 Schwartz Miss B. *(Austria)*
Scott Miss J. *(USA)*
97 Seles Miss M. *(USA)*
Selyutina Miss I. *(Kazakhstan)*
93 Serna Miss M. *(Spain)*
Sfar Miss S. *(Tunisia)*
115 Shaughnessy Miss M. *(USA)*
52 Sidot Miss A-G. *(France)*
24 Smashnova Miss A. *(Israel)*
26 Smith Miss S. *(Great Britain)*
76 Snyder Miss T. *(USA)*
7 Spirlea Miss I. *(Romania)*
88 Srebotnik Miss K. *(Slovenia)*
Steck Miss J. *(South Africa)*
86 Stevenson Miss A. *(USA)*
Stewart Miss B. *(Australia)*
Stubbs Miss R.P. *(Australia)*
121 Suarez Miss P. *(Argentina)*
29 Sugiyama Miss A. *(Japan)*
8 Talaja Miss S. *(Croatia)*
55 Tanasugarn Miss T. *(Thailand)*
Tarabini Miss P. *(Argentina)*
65 Tauziat Miss N. *(France)*
49 Testud Miss S. *(France)*
58 Torrens-Valero Miss C. *(Spain)*
113 Van Roost Mrs D. *(Belgium)*
126 Vavrinec Miss M. *(Switzerland)*
100 Vento Miss M.A. *(Venezuela)*
Vis Miss C.M. *(Netherlands)*
15 Ward Miss J. *(Great Britain)*
87 Wartusch Miss P. *(Austria)*
82 Washington Miss M. *(USA)*
Webb Miss V. *(Canada)*
118 Weingartner Miss M. *(Germany)*
Wild Miss L. *(USA)*
64 Williams Miss S. *(USA)*
32 Williams Miss V. *(USA)*
Woehr Miss J. *(Germany)*
42 Woodroffe Miss L.A. *(Great Britain)*
3 Yi Miss J. *(China P.R.)*
30 Yoshida Miss Y. *(Japan)*
Zavagli Miss M.P. *(Italy)*
53 Zvereva Miss N. *(Belarus)*

GENTLEMEN

Adams D. *(South Africa)*
128 Agassi A. *(USA)*
89 Agenor R. *(Haiti)*
5 Alami K. *(Morocco)*
Albano P. *(Argentina)*
101 Arazi H. *(Morocco)*
Arnold L. *(Argentina)*
52 Arthurs W. *(Australia)*
Aspelin S. *(Sweden)*
Bale L. *(South Africa)*
Barnard M. *(South Africa)*
106 Bastl G. *(Switzerland)*
Behr N. *(Israel)*
54 Berasategui A. *(Spain)*
Bergh F. *(Sweden)*
Bertolini M. *(Italy)*
119 Bhupathi M. *(India)*
14 Bjorkman J. *(Sweden)*
44 Black B. *(Zimbabwe)*
4 Black W. *(Zimbabwe)*
Blake J. *(USA)*
114 Blanco G. *(Spain)*
25 Boutter J. *(France)*
Bowen D. *(USA)*
94 Bower J. *(South Africa)*
Brandi C. *(Italy)*
Broad N. *(Great Britain)*
Bryan B. *(USA)*
Bryan M. *(USA)*
76 Canas G. *(Argentina)*
Carbonell T. *(Spain)*
Carrasco J. *(Spain)*
91 Chang M. *(USA)*
62 Chela J.I. *(Argentina)*
Cibulec T. *(Czech Republic)*
19 Clavet F. *(Spain)*
100 Clement A. *(France)*
Coetzee J. *(South Africa)*
Coupe B. *(USA)*
8 Cowan B. *(Great Britain)*
116 Damm M. *(Czech Republic)*
Davidson J. *(Great Britain)*
De Jager J-L. *(South Africa)*
Delaitre O. *(France)*
79 Delgado J. *(Great Britain)*
127 Dent T. *(USA)*
110 Di Pasquale A. *(France)*
15 Dosedel S. *(Czech Republic)*
Eagle J. *(Australia)*
60 El Aynaoui Y. *(Morocco)*
Ellwood B. *(Australia)*
17 Enqvist T. *(Sweden)*
9 Eschauer W. *(Austria)*
75 Escude N. *(France)*
Etlis G. *(Argentina)*
66 Federer R. *(Switzerland)*
Ferreira E. *(South Africa)*
51 Ferreira W. *(South Africa)*
Florent A. *(Australia)*
Freelove O. *(Great Britain)*
Friedl L. *(Czech Republic)*
35 Fromberg R. *(Australia)*
Galbraith P. *(USA)*
31 Gambill J-M. *(USA)*
Garcia M. *(Argentina)*
29 Gaudenzi A. *(Italy)*
102 Gaudi I. *(Italy)*
92 Gaudio G. *(Argentina)*
7 Gimelstob J. *(USA)*
12 Godwin N. *(South Africa)*
Goellner M-K. *(Germany)*
26 Goldstein P. *(USA)*
122 Golmard J. *(France)*
28 Grosjean S. *(France)*
20 Gumy H. *(Argentina)*
69 Gustafsson M. *(Sweden)*
Haarhuis P. *(Netherlands)*
82 Haas T. *(Germany)*
Haggard C. *(South Africa)*
18 Hantschk M. *(Germany)*
Haygarth B. *(South Africa)*
97 Henman T. *(Great Britain)*
32 Hewitt L. *(Australia)*
Hill M. *(Australia)*
Hilton M.A. *(Great Britain)*
109 Hipfl M. *(Austria)*
Hood M. *(Argentina)*
41 Hrbaty D. *(Slovak Republic)*
120 Huet S. *(France)*
Humphries S. *(USA)*
43 Ilie A. *(Australia)*
99 Ivanisevic G. *(Croatia)*
Iwabuchi S. *(Japan)*
67 Johansson T. *(Sweden)*
Johnson D. *(USA)*
125 Jonsson F. *(Sweden)*
65 Kafelnikov Y. *(Russia)*
81 Kiefer N. *(Germany)*
70 Kilderry P. *(Australia)*
Kim K. *(USA)*
Kitinov A. *(Macedonia)*
Knowles M. *(Bahamas)*
Koenig R. *(South Africa)*
50 Kohlmann M. *(Germany)*
124 Koubek S. *(Austria)*
49 Krajicek R. *(Netherlands)*
Kratzmann A. *(Australia)*
3 Kucera K. *(Slovak Republic)*
96 Kuerten G. *(Brazil)*
Kulti N. *(Sweden)*
Landsberg J. *(Sweden)*
16 Lapentti N. *(Ecuador)*
104 Lareau S. *(Canada)*
Leach R. *(USA)*
57 Lee M. *(Great Britain)*
22 Levy H. *(Israel)*
40 Ljubicic I. *(Croatia)*
6 Llodra M. *(France)*
Lopez-Moron A. *(Spain)*
56 MacLagan M. *(Great Britain)*
Macpherson D. *(Australia)*
MacPhie B. *(USA)*
Malisse X. *(Belgium)*
59 Mantilla F. *(Spain)*
58 Marin J.A. *(Costa Rica)*
Marques N. *(Portugal)*
10 Martin A. *(Spain)*
126 Martin T. *(USA)*
23 Massu N. *(Chile)*
13 Medvedev A. *(Ukraine)*
68 Meligeni F. *(Brazil)*
111 Melzer J. *(Austria)*
71 Mirnyi M. *(Belarus)*
73 Moya C. *(Spain)*
Nargiso D. *(Italy)*
Nelson J. *(Great Britain)*
55 Nestor D. *(Canada)*
Nicolas E. *(Spain)*
33 Norman M. *(Sweden)*
Norval P. *(South Africa)*
37 Novak J. *(Czech Republic)*
Nyborg P. *(Sweden)*
39 O'Brien A. *(USA)*
Olhovskiy A. *(Russia)*
Oncins J. *(Brazil)*
Ondruska M. *(South Africa)*
Orsanic D. *(Argentina)*
Pala P. *(Czech Republic)*
Palmer J. *(USA)*
88 Parmar A. *(Great Britain)*
53 Pavel A. *(Romania)*
Pescosolido S. *(Italy)*
115 Petrovic D. *(Australia)*
112 Philippoussis M. *(Australia)*
64 Pioline C. *(France)*
90 Popp A. *(Germany)*
45 Portas A. *(Spain)*
38 Pozzi G. *(Italy)*
Prieto A. *(Brazil)*
Prieto S. *(Argentina)*
117 Prinosil D. *(Germany)*
Puentes G. *(Spain)*
80 Rafter P. *(Australia)*
Ran E. *(Israel)*
Rikl D. *(Czech Republic)*
Robichaud J. *(Canada)*
107 Rochus C. *(Belgium)*
36 Rochus O. *(Belgium)*
Rodriguez M. *(Argentina)*
85 Rosset M. *(Switzerland)*
48 Rusedski G. *(Great Britain)*
103 Russell M. *(USA)*
63 Ruud C. *(Norway)*
87 Sa A. *(Brazil)*
113 Safin M. *(Russia)*
1 Sampras P. *(USA)*
93 Sanguinetti D. *(Italy)*
Santopadre V. *(Italy)*
30 Santoro F. *(France)*
118 Sargsian S. *(Armenia)*
121 Saulnier C. *(France)*
105 Schalken S. *(Netherlands)*
74 Schuttler R. *(Germany)*
Sell M. *(USA)*
Shimada T. *(Japan)*
77 Siemerink J. *(Netherlands)*
47 Spadea V. *(USA)*
Spencer K. *(Great Britain)*
86 Squillari F. *(Argentina)*
98 Srichaphan P. *(Thailand)*
Stafford G. *(South Africa)*
Stark J. *(USA)*
Stolle S. *(Australia)*
21 Stoltenberg J. *(Australia)*
Suk C. *(Czech Republic)*
Taino E. *(USA)*
27 Tarango J. *(USA)*
Tebbutt M. *(Australia)*
84 Tieleman L. *(Italy)*
108 Tillstrom M. *(Sweden)*
Tramacchi P. *(Australia)*
72 Ulihrach B. *(Czech Republic)*
Ullyett K. *(Zimbabwe)*
2 Vanek J. *(Czech Republic)*
Vanhoudt T. *(Belgium)*
Velasco J. *(Spain)*
Vemic D. *(Yugoslavia)*
11 Vicente F. *(Spain)*
83 Vinciguerra A. *(Sweden)*
24 Vinck C. *(Germany)*
Vizner P. *(Czech Republic)*
123 Voinea A. *(Romania)*
61 Voltchkov V. *(Belarus)*
Waite J. *(USA)*
Wakefield M. *(South Africa)*
78 Woodbridge T.A. *(Australia)*
34 Woodforde M. *(Australia)*
95 Woodruff C. *(USA)*
42 Zabaleta M. *(Argentina)*
46 Zib T. *(Czech Republic)*
Zimonjic N. *(Yugoslavia)*

GIRLS

53 Abramovic Miss I. *(Croatia)*
27 Adamczak Miss M. *(Australia)*
7 Arai Miss Y. *(Japan)*
29 Babakova Miss M. *(Slovak Republic)*
42 Baltacha Miss E. *(Great Britain)*
13 Barnes Miss A. *(Great Britain)*
1 Bedanova Miss D. *(Czech Republic)*
21 Berecz Miss B. *(Hungary)*
9 Beygelzimer Miss Y. *(Ukraine)*
25 Birnerova Miss E. *(Czech Republic)*
28 Bradley Miss M. *(USA)*
Brown Miss M. *(Great Britain)*
52 Cetkovska Miss P. *(Czech Republic)*
24 Cohen Miss A. *(USA)*
49 Collin Miss H. *(Great Britain)*
8 Dlhopolcova Miss L. *(Slovak Republic)*
59 Dowse Miss M. *(Australia)*
41 Dulko Miss G. *(Argentina)*
34 Farr Miss H. *(Great Britain)*
30 Fokina Miss G. *(Russia)*
Fritz-Krockow Miss M. *(Japan)*
16 Gaspar Miss I. *(Romania)*
14 Grier Miss C. *(Great Britain)*
51 Harkleroad Miss A. *(USA)*
Hawkins Miss A. *(Great Britain)*
31 Hewitt Miss J. *(Australia)*
47 Iijima Miss K. *(Japan)*
19 Jolk Miss S. *(Germany)*
32 Kapros Miss A. *(Hungary)*
26 Keothavong Miss A. *(Great Britain)*
60 Kriz Miss N. *(Australia)*
57 Kurhajcova Miss L. *(Slovak Republic)*
23 Ljukovcan Miss R. *(Yugoslavia)*
45 Llewellyn Miss R. *(Great Britain)*
Lopez Miss L. *(Mexico)*
4 Lopez Miss M.J. *(Mexico)*
37 Maes Miss C. *(Belgium)*
12 Mattek Miss B. *(USA)*
48 Mikaelian Miss M. *(Armenia)*
5 Mojzis Miss A. *(South Africa)*
63 Mortello Miss G. *(Italy)*
38 Nakamura Miss A. *(Japan)*
35 Nemeth Miss T. *(Hungary)*
58 O'Connor Miss T. *(New Zealand)*
22 O'Donoghue Miss J. *(Great Britain)*
11 Pandzic Miss J. *(Croatia)*
39 Penkova Miss M. *(Bulgaria)*
64 Perebiynis Miss T. *(Ukraine)*
18 Reyes Miss Z. *(Mexico)*
17 Salerni Miss M.E. *(Argentina)*
56 Schaul Miss C. *(Luxembourg)*
50 Schneider Miss M. *(Poland)*
3 Smith Miss J. *(Great Britain)*
46 Somers Miss I. *(Netherlands)*
20 Stosur Miss S. *(Australia)*
54 Tarjan Miss R. *(Germany)*
55 Tidemand Miss C. *(Norway)*
61 Torres Miss M. *(Mexico)*
62 Trinder Miss N. *(Great Britain)*
43 Valdes Miss E. *(Mexico)*
10 Van Den Knaap Miss L. *(Netherlands)*
Vesenjak Miss M. *(Slovenia)*
44 Vesenjak Miss U. *(Slovenia)*
2 Vinci Miss R. *(Italy)*
40 Voracova Miss R. *(Czech Republic)*
36 Voskoboeva Miss G. *(Russia)*
6 Vymetal Miss K. *(Great Britain)*
Webley-Smith Miss E. *(Great Britain)*
33 Wheeler Miss C. *(Australia)*
15 Widjaja Miss A. *(Indonesia)*
Wright Miss S. *(Great Britain)*

BOYS

16 Abel M. *(Germany)*
38 Abougzir Y. *(USA)*
39 Alver O. *(Norway)*
Amritraj P. *(USA)*
48 Ancic M. *(Croatia)*
27 Balzekas A. *(Lithuania)*
Bamford N. *(Great Britain)*
23 Banks A. *(Great Britain)*
14 Beck K. *(Slovak Republic)*
12 Bloomfield R. *(Great Britain)*
47 Bohli S. *(Switzerland)*
22 Capuccio G-C. *(Venezuela)*
34 Childs L. *(Great Britain)*
10 Coene D. *(Belgium)*
33 Cruciat A. *(Romania)*
52 Davis T. *(USA)*
32 Dernovskyy A. *(Ukraine)*
26 Emery M. *(USA)*
64 Enev T. *(Bulgaria)*
25 Falla A. *(Colombia)*
Flanagan I. *(Great Britain)*
63 Groenfeld B. *(Germany)*
62 Harboe P. *(Chile)*
53 Hernandez J. *(Mexico)*
17 Johansson J. *(Sweden)*
61 Karanusic R. *(Croatia)*
18 Kennedy A. *(Australia)*
51 Khumalo D. *(Zimbabwe)*
30 Klaasen R. *(South Africa)*
41 Kokta M. *(Czech Republic)*
45 Kondo H. *(Japan)*
49 Kracman A. *(Slovenia)*
29 Kubot L. *(Poland)*
44 Lapentti G. *(Ecuador)*
60 Lewis C. *(Great Britain)*
Lockwood S. *(Great Britain)*
57 Lu Y-H. *(Chinese Taipei)*
20 Lukaev R. *(Bulgaria)*
55 Madjarovski D. *(Yugoslavia)*
1 Mahut N. *(France)*
3 Maigret J. *(France)*
46 Marx P. *(Germany)*
13 Matijevic A. *(Croatia)*
36 Medina J. *(Venezuela)*
35 Mirzadeh H. *(USA)*
6 Mitchell S. *(South Africa)*
31 Moukhometov P. *(Russia)*
11 Munoz D. *(Spain)*
15 Nelson J. *(Great Britain)*
42 Nomdo P-J. *(South Africa)*
7 Pocock T. *(Great Britain)*
4 Posada O. *(Venezuela)*
54 Radovanovich L. *(New Zealand)*
5 Rea S. *(New Zealand)*
Reid T. *(Australia)*
50 Riby B. *(Great Britain)*
43 Russell R. *(Jamaica)*
59 Segodo A. *(Benin)*
58 Smith M. *(Great Britain)*
24 Soares B. *(Brazil)*
28 Sofyan H. *(Armenia)*
19 Stadler S. *(Germany)*
37 Stelko I. *(Croatia)*
8 Tipsavevic J. *(Yugoslavia)*
9 Valent R. *(Switzerland)*
56 Villagran C. *(Argentina)*
40 Vliegen K. *(Belgium)*
21 Wang Y. *(Chinese Taipei)*
2 Wiespeiner S. *(Austria)*

Bold figures denote position in Singles Draw

Holder: P.Sampras

The winner becomes the holder, for the year only, of the CHALLENGE CUP presented by The All England Lawn Tennis and Croquet Club. The winner receives a silver replica of the Challenge Cup. A silver salver is presented to the runner-up and a bronze medal to each defeated semi-finalist.

First Round

1. **P.Sampras [1]** (USA)
2. J.Vanek (CZE)
3. K.Kucera (SVK)
(L) 4. W.Black (ZIM)
5. K.Alami (MAR)
(Q) 6. M.Llodra (FRA)
7. J.Gimelstob (USA)
(W) 8. B.Cowan (GBR)
(L) 9. W.Eschauer (AUT)
10. A.Martin (ESP)
11. F.Vicente (ESP)
(Q) 12. N.Godwin (RSA)
13. A.Medvedev (UKR)
14. J.Bjorkman (SWE)
15. S.Dosedel (CZE)
16. **N.Lapentti [16]** (ECU)
17. **T.Enqvist [9]** (SWE)
18. M.Hantschk (GER)
19. F.Clavet (ESP)
20. H.Gumy (ARG)
21. J.Stoltenberg (AUS)
(Q) 22. H.Levy (ISR)
23. N.Massu (CHI)
(Q) 24. C.Vinck (GER)
25. J.Boutter (FRA)
26. P.Goldstein (USA)
27. J.Tarango (USA)
28. S.Grosjean (FRA)
29. A.Gaudenzi (ITA)
30. F.Santoro (FRA)
31. J-M.Gambill (USA)
32. **L.Hewitt [7]** (AUS)
33. **M.Norman [3]** (SWE)
(W) 34. M.Woodforde (AUS)
35. R.Fromberg (AUS)
(Q) 36. O.Rochus (BEL)
37. J.Novak (CZE)
38. G.Pozzi (ITA)
(Q) 39. A.O'Brien (USA)
40. I.Ljubicic (CRO)
41. D.Hrbaty (SVK)
42. M.Zabaleta (ARG)
43. A.Ilie (AUS)
44. B.Black (ZIM)
45. A.Portas (ESP)
46. T.Zib (CZE)
47. V.Spadea (USA)
48. **G.Rusedski [14]** (GBR)
49. **R.Krajicek [11]** (NED)
(L) 50. M.Kohlmann (GER)
51. W.Ferreira (RSA)
52. W.Arthurs (AUS)
53. A.Pavel (ROM)
54. A.Berasategui (ESP)
55. D.Nestor (CAN)
(W) 56. M.MacLagan (GBR)
(W) 57. M.Lee (GBR)
58. J.A.Marin (CRC)
59. F.Mantilla (ESP)
60. Y.El Aynaoui (MAR)
(Q) 61. V.Voltchkov (BLR)
62. J.I.Chela (ARG)
63. C.Ruud (NOR)
64. **C.Pioline [6]** (FRA)
65. **Y.Kafelnikov [5]** (RUS)
66. R.Federer (SUI)
67. T.Johansson (SWE)
68. F.Meligeni (BRA)
69. M.Gustafsson (SWE)
(Q) 70. P.Kilderry (AUS)
71. M.Mirnyi (BLR)
72. B.Ulihrach (CZE)
73. C.Moya (ESP)
74. R.Schuttler (GER)
75. N.Escude (FRA)
76. G.Canas (ARG)
77. J.Siemerink (NED)
(W) 78. T.A.Woodbridge (AUS)
(W) 79. J.Delgado (GBR)
80. **P.Rafter [12]** (AUS)
81. **N.Kiefer [13]** (GER)
82. T.Haas (GER)
83. A.Vinciguerra (SWE)
84. L.Tieleman (ITA)
85. M.Rosset (SUI)
86. F.Squillari (ARG)
87. A.Sa (BRA)
(W) 88. A.Parmar (GBR)
89. R.Agenor (HAI)
90. A.Popp (GER)
91. M.Chang (USA)
92. G.Gaudio (ARG)
93. D.Sanguinetti (ITA)
(Q) 94. J.Bower (RSA)
95. C.Woodruff (USA)
96. **G.Kuerten [4]** (BRA)
97. **T.Henman [8]** (GBR)
98. P.Srichaphan (THA)
99. G.Ivanisevic (CRO)
100. A.Clement (FRA)
101. H.Arazi (MAR)
(Q) 102. I.Gaudi (ITA)
(Q) 103. M.Russell (USA)
(L) 104. S.Lareau (CAN)
105. S.Schalken (NED)
106. G.Bastl (SUI)
107. C.Rochus (BEL)
108. M.Tillstrom (SWE)
109. M.Hipfl (AUT)
110. A.Di Pasquale (FRA)
(Q) 111. J.Melzer (AUT)
112. **M.Philippoussis [10]** (AUS)
113. **M.Safin [15]** (RUS)
114. G.Blanco (ESP)
(Q) 115. D.Petrovic (AUS)
116. M.Damm (CZE)
(Q) 117. D.Prinosil (GER)
118. S.Sargsian (ARM)
(W) 119. M.Bhupathi (IND)
(Q) 120. S.Huet (FRA)
(L) 121. C.Saulnier (FRA)
122. J.Golmard (FRA)
123. A.Voinea (ROM)
124. S.Koubek (AUT)
(L) 125. F.Jonsson (SWE)
126. T.Martin (USA)
(Q) 127. T.Dent (USA)
128. **A.Agassi [2]** (USA)

Second Round

- **P.Sampras [1]** 6/4 6/4 6/2
- K.Kucera 6/2 6/2 6/4
- M.Llodra 6/3 6/3 6/1
- J.Gimelstob 6/3 6/4 6/7(5) 6/2
- A.Martin 6/4 6/4 3/6 6/2
- N.Godwin 6/7(6) 6/1 3/6 6/2 8/6
- J.Bjorkman
- S.Dosedel 6/3 6/2 0/6 6/1
- **T.Enqvist [9]** 6/1 6/4 6/2
- F.Clavet 6/3 6/3 6/3
- H.Levy 6/3 2/6 6/7(3) 6/4 6/4
- C.Vinck 7/5 4/6 7/6(6) 3/6 6/3
- P.Goldstein 7/6(1) 6/3 6/4
- J.Tarango 7/6(5) 3/6 6/4 6/4
- F.Santoro 6/3 6/2 6/2
- J-M.Gambill 6/3 6/2 7/5
- **M.Norman [3]** 6/4 6/2 2/0 Ret'd
- O.Rochus 4/6 6/3 3/6 7/6(4) 6/4
- G.Pozzi 6/3 6/4 3/6 6/1
- A.O'Brien 5/7 6/1 7/5 7/6(4)
- D.Hrbaty 6/4 6/2 7/5
- B.Black 6/3 5/7 7/6(4) 6/0
- A.Portas 6/3 6/4 6/4
- V.Spadea 6/3 6/7(5) 6/3 6/7(8) 9/7
- **R.Krajicek [11]** 3/6 6/1 6/4 7/6(3)
- W.Ferreira 6/7(6) 6/3 7/6(5) 6/1
- A.Pavel 6/0 6/4 6/2
- D.Nestor 4/6 7/6(3) 6/2 6/4
- M.Lee 6/2 6/4 7/6(3)
- Y.El Aynaoui 7/6(5) 6/3 6/4
- V.Voltchkov 6/7(5) 6/3 3/6 6/3 6/0
- **C.Pioline [6]** 7/6(4) 6/1 4/6 6/3
- **Y.Kafelnikov [5]** 7/5 7/5 7/6(6)
- T.Johansson 6/4 6/7(5) 6/2 6/4
- M.Gustafsson 6/4 6/2 6/4
- M.Mirnyi 6/2 4/0 Ret'd
- R.Schuttler 6/3 6/7(5) 6/1
- N.Escude 4/6 6/4 6/1 6/2
- T.A.Woodbridge 6/4 3/6 7/6(4) 6/2
- **P.Rafter [12]** 6/3 7/6(7) 6/1
- T.Haas 5/7 6/4 6/2 6/3
- A.Vinciguerra 7/6(4) 6/1 6/7(7) 6/2
- M.Rosset 7/5 6/3 7/6(4)
- A.Parmar 6/7(2) 6/3 4/6 6/2 6/3
- A.Popp 0/6 7/5 7/6(10) 6/2
- M.Chang 6/2 6/3 6/2
- J.Bower 6/3 7/6(1) 4/6 7/6(1)
- **G.Kuerten [4]** 6/4 6/7(5) 7/5 7/6(5)
- **T.Henman [8]** 5/7 6/3 6/1 6/3
- A.Clement 6/3 3/6 6/3 6/4
- H.Arazi 6/2 6/4 6/0
- S.Lareau 7/6(6) 6/2 1/6 6/2
- S.Schalken 6/2 6/4 6/2
- C.Rochus 4/6 7/6(7) 6/2 4/6 6/1
- A.Di Pasquale 4/6 6/4 6/4 6/7(5) 6/1
- **M.Philippoussis [10]** 6/4 7/6(3) 5/7 6/4
- **M.Safin [15]** 7/6(2) 6/3 6/4
- M.Damm 6/1 6/4 6/1
- D.Prinosil 2/6 6/1 6/2 6/4
- S.Huet 6/7(5) 6/3 7/6(4) 6/1
- J.Golmard 7/5 6/4 6/4
- S.Koubek 3/3 Ret'd
- T.Martin 7/6(7) 7/6(1) 6/2
- **A.Agassi [2]** 2/6 6/3 6/0 4/0 Ret'd

Third Round

- **P.Sampras [1]** 7/6(9) 3/6 6/3 6/4
- J.Gimelstob 7/6(3) 6/3 6/4
- N.Godwin 7/5 6/4 6/3
- J.Bjorkman 6/4 6/3 6/0
- **T.Enqvist [9]** 7/6(2) 7/6(6) 7/5
- C.Vinck 6/4 7/6(2) 7/5
- P.Goldstein 3/6 6/2 5/7 6/2 12/10
- J-M.Gambill 4/6 6/2 6/2
- O.Rochus 6/4 2/6 6/4 6/7(4) 6/1
- G.Pozzi 7/6(6) 6/3 6/4
- B.Black 6/3 7/5 6/2
- A.Portas 6/4 6/3 6/3
- W.Ferreira 5/7 6/3 6/3 7/6(3)
- A.Pavel 7/6(6) 7/5 4/6 6/0
- Y.El Aynaoui 6/7(7) 6/2 6/2 6/2
- V.Voltchkov 6/3 6/3 2/6 3/6 6/4
- T.Johansson 6/1 7/6(0) 6/4
- M.Gustafsson 6/4 6/3 6/1
- R.Schuttler 6/4 7/6(3) 6/7(5)
- **P.Rafter [12]** 6/3 6/3 6/4
- T.Haas 6/3 7/6(3) 6/3
- M.Rosset 7/6(4) 7/5 6/3
- A.Popp 7/6(5) 4/6 6/7(3) 6/3 8/6
- **G.Kuerten [4]** 6/4 6/4 7/5
- **T.Henman [8]** 6/4 6/4 6/4
- H.Arazi 6/3 3/6 6/7(6) 6/4 9/7
- S.Schalken 6/4 6/3 6/0
- **M.Philippoussis [10]** 4/6 7/6(0) 6/3 6/0
- M.Damm 7/5 7/6(4) 6/3
- D.Prinosil 6/4 2/6 6/1 6/2
- J.Golmard 7/6(4) 4/6 6/1 6/2
- **A.Agassi [2]** 6/4 2/6 7/6(3) 2/6 10/8

Fourth Round

- **P.Sampras [1]** 2/6 6/4 6/2 6/2
- J.Bjorkman 6/3 6/4 6/4
- **T.Enqvist [9]** 6/3 6/7(4) 2/6 6/3 6/3
- J-M.Gambill 7/6(10) 6/2 6/2
- G.Pozzi 6/3 3/6 7/6(3) 6/2
- B.Black 6/2 6/0 6/4
- W.Ferreira 3/6 7/6(3) 7/5 6/3
- V.Voltchkov 7/6(4) 7/5 7/6(4)
- T.Johansson 6/7(3) 7/6(1) 6/4 5/7 6/3
- **P.Rafter [12]** 6/2 7/6(2) 6/3
- M.Rosset 6/4 3/6 6/3 3/6 9/7
- A.Popp 7/6(6) 6/2 6/1
- **T.Henman [8]** 6/3 6/3 6/3
- **M.Philippoussis [10]** 4/6 6/3 6/7(7) 7/6(4) 20/18
- D.Prinosil 7/6(2) 3/6 7/6(0) 6/4
- **A.Agassi [2]** 6/4 6/3 6/3

Quarter-Finals

- **P.Sampras [1]** 6/3 6/2 7/5
- J-M.Gambill 7/6(5) 3/6 6/3 6/4
- B.Black 4/6 7/6(5) 6/2 6/4
- V.Voltchkov 6/3 6/4 7/6(0)
- **P.Rafter [12]** 6/3 6/4 6/7(4) 6/1
- A.Popp 6/1 6/4 3/6 6/1
- **M.Philippoussis [10]** 6/1 5/7 6/7(9) 6/3 6/4
- **A.Agassi [2]** 7/6(4) 7/5 4/6 6/3

Semi-Finals

- **P.Sampras [1]** 6/4 6/7(4) 6/4 6/4
- V.Voltchkov 7/6(2) 7/6(2) 6/4
- **P.Rafter [12]** 6/3 6/2 7/6(1)
- **A.Agassi [2]** 7/6(4) 6/3 6/4

Final

- **P.Sampras [1]** 7/6(4) 6/2 6/4
- **P.Rafter [12]** 7/5 4/6 7/5 4/6 6/3

Champion

P.Sampras [1] 6/7(10) 7/6(5) 6/4 6/2

Heavy type denotes seeded players. The figure in brackets against names denotes the order in which they have been seeded. (W) = Wild card. (Q) = Qualifier. (L) = Lucky loser.

The matches are the best of five sets

Holders: M.Bhupathi and L.Paes

The winners become the holders, for the year only, of the CHALLENGE CUPS presented by the OXFORD UNIVERSITY LAWN TENNIS CLUB and the late SIR HERBERT WILBERFORCE respectively. The winners receive silver replicas of the two Challenge Cups. A silver salver is presented to each of the runners-up, and a bronze medal to each defeated semi-finalist.

First Round	Second Round	Third Round	Quarter-Finals	Semi-Finals	Final

1. **T.A.Woodbridge** (AUS) & **M.Woodforde** (AUS) ....[1]
2. J-M.Gambill (USA) & S.Humphries (USA) ....

  T.A.Woodbridge & M.Woodforde [1] 6/2 6/3 6/2

(W) 3. J.Delgado (GBR) & M.Lee (GBR)
4. T.Shimada (JPN) & M.Wakefield (RSA)

  T.Shimada & M.Wakefield ....7/6(2) 6/3 6/1

T.A.Woodbridge & M.Woodforde [1] ....7/6(5) 7/6(3) 4/6 6/3

5. M.Bertolini (ITA) & C.Brandi (ITA)
(W) 6. B.Cowan (GBR) & K.Spencer (GBR)

  M.Bertolini & C.Brandi 6/4 6/3 7/5

(W) 7. N.Broad (GBR) & A.Parmar (GBR)
8. **J.Eagle** (AUS) & **A.Florent** (AUS) ....[15]

  J.Eagle & A.Florent [15] ....6/4 4/6 7/6(3) 3/6 6/3

M.Bertolini & C.Brandi ....6/4 7/6(4) 6/7(4) 3/6 6/3

T.A.Woodbridge & M.Woodforde [1] 6/4 6/3 6/3

9. **S.Lareau** (CAN) & **D.Nestor** (CAN) ....[9]
10. M.Barnard (RSA) & C.Haggard (RSA)

  S.Lareau & D.Nestor [9] 4/6 6/3 4/6 6/1

(Q) 11. S.Pescosolido (ITA) & V.Santopadre (ITA)
12. G.Stafford (RSA) & P.Tramacchi (AUS)

  S.Pescosolido & V.Santopadre ....6/3 6/7(2) 6/3 6/2

S.Lareau & D.Nestor [9] ....6/1 6/4 6/7(2) 6/2

(W) 13. M.A.Hilton (GBR) & J.Nelson (GBR)
14. P.Pala (CZE) & P.Vizner (CZE)

  P.Pala & P.Vizner ....7/5 6/4 6/7(7) 7/6(4)

15. G.Etlis (ARG) & M.Rodriguez (ARG)
16. **J.Novak** (CZE) & **D.Rikl** (CZE) ....[8]

  J.Novak & D.Rikl [8] 4/6 6/4 6/3 3/6 9/7

J.Novak & D.Rikl [8] 6/1 6/2 6/4

S.Lareau & D.Nestor [9] ....6/4 6/3 7/6(2)

17. **A.O'Brien** (USA) & **J.Palmer** (USA) ....[3]
18. T.Cibulec (CZE) & L.Friedl (CZE)

  A.O'Brien & J.Palmer [3] 6/0 6/2 6/4

(W) 19. J.Davidson (GBR) & O.Freelove (GBR)
20. P.Kilderry (AUS) & A.Martin (ESP)

  P.Kilderry & A.Martin ....6/4 6/7(4) 7/5

A.O'Brien & J.Palmer [3] 6/0 4/6 4/6

(Q) 21. N.Behr (ISR) & S.Iwabuchi (JPN)
22. J.Oncins (BRA) & C.Suk (CZE)

  J.Oncins & C.Suk 1/6 6/1 6/4 6/4

23. D.Hrbaty (SVK) & G.Kuerten (BRA)
24. **D.Johnson** (USA) & **P.Norval** (RSA) ....[13]

  D.Johnson & P.Norval [13] ....6/7(4) 7/6(4) 2/1 Ret'd

J.Oncins & C.Suk 6/4 3/6 2/6 6/4 8/6

A.O'Brien & J.Palmer [3] ....4/6 3/7 7/5 6/7(2) 7/5

25. **N.Kulti** (SWE) & **M.Tillstrom** (SWE) ....[11]
26. D.Macpherson (AUS) & M.Tebbutt (AUS)

  N.Kulti & M.Tillstrom [11] 7/5 6/3 6/1

(Q) 27. J.Robichaud (CAN) & M.Sell (USA)
28. M-K.Goellner (GER) & J.Siemerink (NED)

  M-K.Goellner & J.Siemerink ....7/6(4) 3/6 2/6 7/5 10/8

N.Kulti & M.Tillstrom [11] ....7/6(3) 7/6(2) 7/6(4)

29. M.Llodra (FRA) & D.Nargiso (ITA)
30. A.Kitinov (MKD) & D.Vemic (YUG)

  M.Llodra & D.Nargiso ....7/6(4) 6/4 6/4

31. L.Arnold (ARG) & D.Orsanic (ARG)
32. **J.Bjorkman** (SWE) & **B.Black** (ZIM) ....[5]

  J.Bjorkman & B.Black [5] ....6/4 7/6(4) 6/3

J.Bjorkman & B.Black [5] ....7/6(6) 7/5 3/6 6/1

N.Kulti & M.Tillstrom [11] ....7/6(3) 6/3 7/6(7)

33. **D.Adams** (RSA) & **J-L.De Jager** (RSA) ....[6]
34. S.Aspelin (SWE) & J.Landsberg (SWE)

  D.Adams & J-L.De Jager [6] ....7/6(5) 3/6 6/3 5/7 6/4

35. N.Marques (POR) & T.Vanhoudt (BEL)
36. R.Koenig (RSA) & A.Olhovskiy (RUS)

  R.Koenig & A.Olhovskiy ....6/7(2) 7/6(7) 6/3 7/6(4)

D.Adams & J-L.De Jager [6] ....7/6(7) 6/4 6/7(2) 6/4

37. P.Galbraith (USA) & B.MacPhie (USA)
38. B.Bryan (USA) & M.Bryan (USA)

  P.Galbraith & B.MacPhie ....6/4 6/4 7/6(4)

39. W.Arthurs (AUS) & B.Ellwood (AUS)
40. **W.Black** (ZIM) & **K.Ullyett** (ZIM) ....[12]

  W.Arthurs & B.Ellwood 5/7 7/5 7/5 6/3

W.Arthurs & B.Ellwood ....4/6 6/3 6/4 7/6(4)

D.Adams & J-L.De Jager [6] 3/6 7/5 7/5 6/3

41. **J.Gimelstob** (USA) & **M.Knowles** (BAH) ....[14]
42. M.Mirnyi (BLR) & N.Zimonjic (YUG)

  J.Gimelstob & M.Knowles [14] 6/3 6/2 6/4

43. D.Bowen (USA) & B.Coupe (USA)
44. A.Prieto (BRA) & E.Ran (ISR)

  A.Prieto & E.Ran ....6/3 2/6 7/6(2) 4/6 6/3

J.Gimelstob & M.Knowles [14] 7/5 6/3 6/4

45. N.Godwin (RSA) & M.Hill (AUS)
46. M.Rosset (SUI) & J.Tarango (USA)

  M.Rosset & J.Tarango ....4/6 7/6(5) 7/6(5) 6/3

47. P.Albano (ARG) & N.Lapentti (ECU)
48. **E.Ferreira** (RSA) & **R.Leach** (USA) ....[4]

  E.Ferreira & R.Leach [4] ....7/6(4) 6/2 6/4

E.Ferreira & R.Leach [4] 4/6 3/6 6/0 6/1

E.Ferreira & R.Leach [4] 6/3 6/4 6/4

49. **M.Damm** (CZE) & **W.Ferreira** (RSA) ....[7]
50. L.Bale (RSA) & M.Ondruska (RSA)

  M.Damm & W.Ferreira [7] ....7/6(5) 6/4 4/6 6/2

51. R.Federer (SUI) & A.Kratzmann (AUS)
(Q) 52. J.Blake (USA) & K.Kim (USA)

  R.Federer & A.Kratzmann ....6/3 6/7(4) 6/2 6/7(3) 6/4

R.Federer & A.Kratzmann ....7/6(5) 6/2 3/6 6/4

53. E.Nicolas (ESP) & G.Puentes (ESP)
54. F.Bergh (SWE) & P.Nyborg (SWE)

  F.Bergh & P.Nyborg ....6/3 7/6(5) 6/4

55. M.Hood (ARG) & S.Prieto (ARG)
56. **M.Bhupathi** (IND) & **D.Prinosil** (GER) ....[10]

  M.Bhupathi & D.Prinosil [10] 6/3 6/2 6/4

M.Bhupathi & D.Prinosil [10] ....6/4 7/6(6) 4/6 7/6(11)

R.Federer & A.Kratzmann ....7/6(2) 6/4 6/4

57. **T.Carbonell** (ESP) & **M.Garcia** (ARG) ....[16]
58. O.Delaitre (FRA) & F.Santoro (FRA)

  O.Delaitre & F.Santoro 6/2 6/4 3/6 7/5

59. A.Lopez-Moron (ESP) & A.Portas (ESP)
60. J.Coetzee (RSA) & B.Haygarth (RSA)

  J.Coetzee & B.Haygarth ....6/3 6/1 6/7(2) 6/3

O.Delaitre & F.Santoro 3/6 6/3 6/2 6/2

61. P.Goldstein (USA) & J.Waite (USA)
62. J.Carrasco (ESP) & J.Velasco (ESP)

  P.Goldstein & J.Waite ....6/4 6/4 5/7 7/6(5) 6/2

P.Haarhuis & S.Stolle [2] 6/2 6/2 6/4

63. J.Stark (USA) & E.Taino (USA)
64. **P.Haarhuis** (NED) & **S.Stolle** (AUS) ....[2]

  P.Haarhuis & S.Stolle [2] ....6/7(2) 7/6(7) 6/4 6/3

P.Haarhuis & S.Stolle [2] ....6/3 7/6(3) 7/5

Quarter-Finals / Semi-Finals / Final

T.A.Woodbridge & M.Woodforde [1] ....6/3 6/7(4) 4/6 6/3 8/6

N.Kulti & M.Tillstrom [11] 4/6 3/6 6/3 6/3

D.Adams & J-L.De Jager [6] ....6/7(5) 6/7(3) 7/6(4) 7/6(7) 8/6

P.Haarhuis & S.Stolle [2] ....6/7(5) 5/7 7/6(2) 6/2 6/2

T.A.Woodbridge & M.Woodforde [1] ....6/4 7/6(2) 6/2

P.Haarhuis & S.Stolle [2] ....6/4 7/6(5) 6/7(4) 6/4

T.A.Woodbridge & M.Woodforde [1] 6/3 6/4 6/1

Heavy type denotes seeded players. The figure in brackets against names denotes the order in which they have been seeded. (W) = Wild card. (Q) = Qualifier. (L) = Lucky loser.

The matches are the best of five sets

The winner becomes the holder, for the year only, of the CHALLENGE TROPHY presented by The All England Lawn Tennis and Croquet Club. The winner receives a silver replica of the Trophy. A silver salver is presented to the runner-up and a bronze medal to each defeated semi-finalist.

Holder: Miss L.A.Davenport

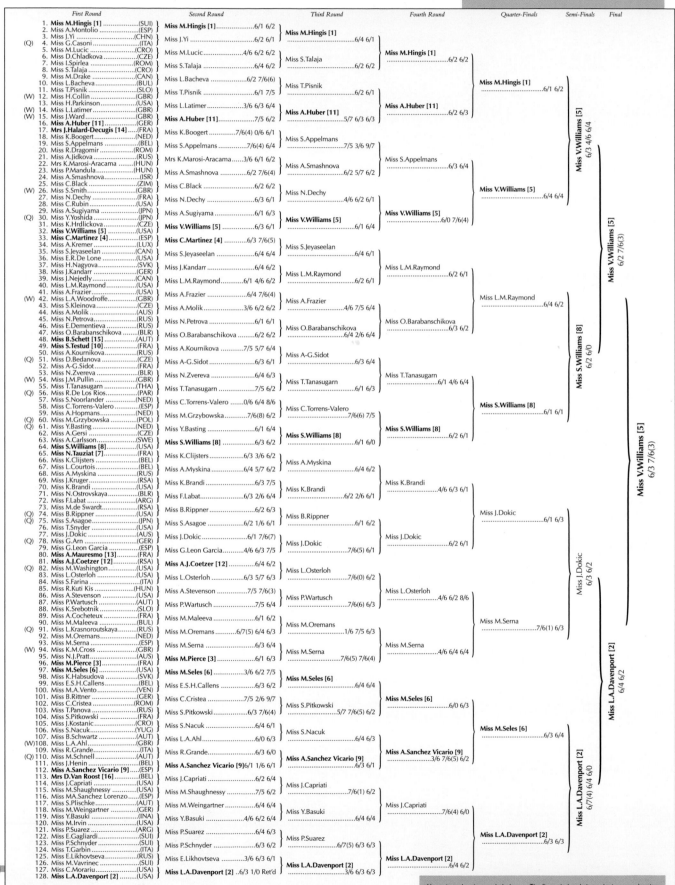

First Round	Second Round	Third Round	Fourth Round	Quarter-Finals	Semi-Finals	Final
1. **Miss M.Hingis [1]** (SUI)	**Miss M.Hingis [1]** 6/1 6/2					
2. Miss A.Montolio (ESP)		**Miss M.Hingis [1]**				
3. Miss J.Yi (CHN)	Miss J.Yi 6/2 6/1	6/4 6/1				
(Q) 4. Miss G.Casoni (ITA)			**Miss M.Hingis [1]**			
5. Miss M.Lucic (CRO)	Miss M.Lucic 4/6 6/2 6/2		6/2 6/2			
6. Miss D.Chladkova (CZE)		Miss S.Talaja				
7. Miss I.Spirlea (ROM)	Miss S.Talaja 6/4 6/2	6/2 6/2				
8. Miss S.Talaja (CRO)				**Miss M.Hingis [1]**		
9. Miss M.Drake (CAN)	Miss L.Bacheva 6/2 7/6(6)			6/1 6/2		
10. Miss L.Bacheva (BUL)		Miss T.Pisnik				
11. Miss T.Pisnik (SLO)	Miss T.Pisnik 6/1 7/5	6/2 6/1				
(W) 12. Miss H.Collin (GBR)			**Miss A.Huber [11]**			
13. Miss H.Parkinson (USA)	Miss L.Latimer 3/6 6/3 6/4		6/2 6/3			
(W) 14. Miss L.Latimer (GBR)		**Miss A.Huber [11]**				
(W) 15. Miss J.Ward (GBR)	**Miss A.Huber [11]** 7/5 6/2	5/7 6/3 6/3				
16. **Miss A.Huber [11]** (GER)					**Miss V.Williams [5]**	
17. Mrs J.Halard-Decugis [14] (FRA)	Miss K.Boogert 7/6(4) 0/6 6/1				6/3 4/6 6/4	
18. Miss K.Boogert (NED)		Miss S.Appelmans				
19. Miss S.Appelmans (BEL)	Miss S.Appelmans 7/6(4) 6/4	7/5 3/6 9/7				
20. Miss R.Dragomir (ROM)			Miss S.Appelmans			
21. Miss A.Jidkova (RUS)	Mrs K.Marosi-Aracama 3/6 6/1 6/2		6/3 6/4			
22. Mrs K.Marosi-Aracama (HUN)		Miss A.Smashnova				
23. Miss P.Mandula (HUN)	Miss A.Smashnova 6/2 7/6(4)	6/2 5/7 6/2				
24. Miss A.Smashnova (ISR)				**Miss V.Williams [5]**		
25. Miss C.Black (ZIM)	Miss C.Black 6/2 6/2			6/4 6/4		
(W) 26. Miss S.Smith (GBR)		Miss N.Dechy				
27. Miss N.Dechy (FRA)	Miss N.Dechy 6/3 6/1	4/6 6/2 6/1				
28. Miss C.Rubin (USA)			**Miss V.Williams [5]**			
29. Miss A.Sugiyama (JPN)	Miss A.Sugiyama 6/1 6/3		6/1 6/4			
(Q) 30. Miss Y.Yoshida (JPN)		**Miss V.Williams [5]**				
31. Miss K.Hrdlickova (CZE)	**Miss V.Williams [5]** 6/3 6/1	6/0 7/6(4)				
32. **Miss V.Williams [5]** (USA)						**Miss V.Williams [5]**
33. **Miss C.Martinez [4]** (ESP)	**Miss C.Martinez [4]** 6/3 7/6(5)					6/3 7/6(3)
34. Miss A.Kremer (LUX)		Miss S.Jeyaseelan				
35. Miss S.Jeyaseelan (CAN)	Miss S.Jeyaseelan 6/4 6/4	6/4 6/1				
36. Miss E.R.De Lone (USA)			Miss L.M.Raymond			
37. Miss H.Nagyova (SVK)	Miss J.Kandarr 6/4 6/2		6/2 6/1			
38. Miss J.Kandarr (GER)		Miss L.M.Raymond				
39. Miss J.Nejedly (CAN)	Miss L.M.Raymond 6/1 4/6 6/2	6/2 6/1				
40. Miss L.M.Raymond (USA)				Miss L.M.Raymond		
41. Miss A.Frazier (USA)	Miss A.Frazier 6/4 7/6(4)			6/4 6/2		
(W) 42. Miss L.A.Woodroffe (GBR)		Miss A.Frazier				
43. Miss S.Kleinova (CZE)	Miss A.Molik 3/6 6/2 6/2	4/6 7/5 6/4				
44. Miss A.Molik (AUS)			Miss O.Barabanschikova			
45. Miss N.Petrova (RUS)	Miss N.Petrova 6/1 6/1		6/3 6/2			
46. Miss E.Dementieva (RUS)		Miss O.Barabanschikova				
47. Miss O.Barabanschikova (BLR)	Miss O.Barabanschikova 6/2 6/2	6/4 2/6 6/4				
48. **Miss B.Schett [15]** (AUT)				**Miss S.Williams [8]**		
49. **Miss S.Testud [10]** (FRA)	Miss A.Kournikova 7/5 5/7 6/4			6/2 6/0		
50. Miss A.Kournikova (RUS)		Miss A-G.Sidot				
(Q) 51. Miss D.Bedanova (CZE)	Miss A-G.Sidot 6/3 6/1	6/3 6/4				
52. Miss A-G.Sidot (FRA)			Miss T.Tanasugarn			
53. Miss N.Zvereva (BLR)	Miss N.Zvereva 6/4 6/3		6/1 4/6 6/4			
(W) 54. Miss J.M.Pullin (GBR)		Miss T.Tanasugarn				
55. Miss T.Tanasugarn (THA)	Miss T.Tanasugarn 7/5 6/2	6/1 6/3				
(Q) 56. Miss R.De Los Rios (PAR)				**Miss S.Williams [8]**		
57. Miss S.Noorlander (NED)	Miss C.Torrens-Valero 0/6 6/4 8/6			6/1 6/1		
58. Miss C.Torrens-Valero (ESP)		Miss C.Torrens-Valero				
59. Miss A.Hopmans (NED)	Miss M.Grzybowska 7/6(8) 6/2	7/6(6) 7/5				
(Q) 60. Miss M.Grzybowska (POL)			**Miss S.Williams [8]**			
(Q) 61. Miss Y.Basting (NED)	Miss Y.Basting 6/1 6/4		6/2 6/1			
62. Miss A.Gersi (CZE)		**Miss S.Williams [8]**				
63. Miss A.Carlsson (SWE)	**Miss S.Williams [8]** 6/3 6/2	6/1 6/0				
64. **Miss S.Williams [8]** (USA)					**Miss S.Williams [8]**	
65. **Miss N.Tauziat [7]** (FRA)	Miss K.Clijsters 6/3 3/6 6/2				6/2 6/2	
66. Miss K.Clijsters (BEL)		Miss A.Myskina				
67. Miss L.Courtois (BEL)	Miss A.Myskina 6/4 5/7 6/2	6/4 6/2				
68. Miss A.Myskina (RUS)			Miss K.Brandi			
69. Miss J.Kruger (RSA)	Miss K.Brandi 6/3 7/5		4/6 6/3 6/1			
70. Miss K.Brandi (USA)		Miss K.Brandi				
71. Miss N.Ostrovskaya (BLR)	Miss F.Labat 6/3 2/6 6/4	6/2 2/6 6/1				
72. Miss F.Labat (ARG)				Miss J.Dokic		
73. Miss M.de Swardt (RSA)	Miss B.Rippner 6/2 6/3			6/1 6/3		
(Q) 74. Miss B.Rippner (USA)		Miss B.Rippner				
(Q) 75. Miss S.Asagoe (JPN)	Miss S.Asagoe 6/2 1/6 6/1	6/1 6/2				
76. Miss T.Snyder (USA)			Miss J.Dokic			
77. Miss J.Dokic (AUS)	Miss J.Dokic 6/1 7/6(7)		7/6(5) 6/1			
(Q) 78. Miss G.Arn (GER)		Miss J.Dokic				
79. Miss G.Leon Garcia (ESP)	Miss G.Leon Garcia 4/6 6/3 7/5	7/6(5) 6/1				
80. **Miss A.Mauresmo [13]** (FRA)				**Miss J.Dokic**		
81. **Miss A.J.Coetzer [12]** (RSA)	**Miss A.J.Coetzer [12]** 6/4 6/2			6/3 6/2		
(Q) 82. Miss M.Washington (USA)		Miss L.Osterloh				
83. Miss L.Osterloh (USA)	Miss L.Osterloh 6/3 5/7 6/3	7/6(0) 6/2				
84. Miss S.Farina (ITA)			Miss L.Osterloh			
85. Miss R.Kuti Kis (HUN)	Miss A.Stevenson 7/5 7/6(3)		4/6 6/2 8/6			
86. Miss A.Stevenson (USA)		Miss P.Wartusch				
87. Miss P.Wartusch (AUT)	Miss P.Wartusch 7/5 6/4	7/6(6) 6/3				
88. Miss K.Srebotnik (SLO)				Miss M.Serna		
89. Miss A.Cocheteux (FRA)	Miss M.Maleeva 6/1 6/2			7/6(1) 6/3		
90. Miss M.Maleeva (BUL)		Miss M.Oremans				
(Q) 91. Miss L.Krasnoroutskaya (RUS)	Miss M.Oremans 6/7(5) 6/4 6/3	1/6 7/5 6/3				
92. Miss M.Oremans (NED)			Miss M.Serna			
93. Miss M.Serna (ESP)	Miss M.Serna 6/3 6/4		4/6 6/4 6/4			
(W) 94. Miss K.M.Cross (GBR)		Miss M.Serna				
95. Miss N.J.Pratt (AUS)	**Miss M.Pierce [3]** 6/1 6/3	7/6(5) 7/6(4)				
96. **Miss M.Pierce [3]** (FRA)					**Miss L.A.Davenport [2]**	
97. **Miss M.Seles [6]** (USA)	**Miss M.Seles [6]** 3/6 6/2 7/5				6/4 6/2	
98. Miss K.Habsudova (SVK)		**Miss M.Seles [6]**				
99. Miss E.S.H.Callens (BEL)	Miss E.S.H.Callens 6/3 6/2	6/4 6/4				
100. Miss M.A.Vento (VEN)			**Miss M.Seles [6]**			
101. Miss B.Rittner (GER)	Miss C.Cristea 7/5 2/6 9/7		6/0 6/3			
102. Miss C.Cristea (ROM)		Miss S.Pitkowski				
103. Miss T.Panova (RUS)	Miss S.Pitkowski 6/3 7/6(4)	5/7 7/6(5) 6/2				
104. Miss S.Pitkowski (CRO)				**Miss M.Seles [6]**		
105. Miss J.Kostanic (CRO)	Miss S.Nacuk 6/4 6/1			6/3 6/4		
106. Miss S.Nacuk (YUG)		Miss S.Nacuk				
107. Miss B.Schwartz (AUT)	Miss L.A.Ahl 6/0 6/3	6/4 6/3				
(W)108. Miss L.A.Ahl (GBR)			**Miss A.Sanchez Vicario [9]**			
109. Miss R.Grande (ITA)	Miss R.Grande 6/3 6/0		3/6 7/6(5) 6/2			
(Q) 110. Miss M.Schnell (AUT)		**Miss A.Sanchez Vicario [9]**				
111. Miss J.Henin (BEL)	**Miss A.Sanchez Vicario [9]** 6/1 1/6 6/1	6/3 6/4				
112. **Miss A.Sanchez Vicario [9]** (ESP)				**Miss L.A.Davenport [2]**		
113. **Mrs D.Van Roost [16]** (BEL)	Miss J.Capriati 6/2 6/4			6/7(4) 6/4 6/0		
114. Miss J.Capriati (USA)		Miss J.Capriati				
115. Miss M.Shaughnessy (USA)	Miss M.Shaughnessy 7/5 6/4	7/6(1) 6/2				
116. Miss MA.Sanchez Lorenzo (ESP)			Miss J.Capriati			
117. Miss S.Plischke (AUT)	Miss M.Weingartner 6/4 6/4		7/6(4) 6/0			
118. Miss M.Weingartner (GER)		Miss Y.Basuki				
119. Miss Y.Basuki (INA)	Miss Y.Basuki 4/6 6/2 6/4	6/4 6/4				
120. Miss M.Irvin (USA)				**Miss L.A.Davenport [2]**		
121. Miss P.Suarez (ARG)	Miss P.Suarez 6/4 6/3			6/3 6/3		
122. Miss E.Gagliardi (SUI)		Miss P.Suarez				
123. Miss P.Schnyder (SUI)	Miss P.Schnyder 6/3 6/2	6/7(5) 6/3 6/3				
124. Miss T.Garbin (ITA)			**Miss L.A.Davenport [2]**			
125. Miss E.Likhovtseva (RUS)	Miss E.Likhovtseva 3/6 6/3 6/1		6/4 6/2			
126. Miss M.Vavrinec (SUI)		**Miss L.A.Davenport [2]**				
127. Miss C.Morariu (USA)	**Miss L.A.Davenport [2]** 6/3 1/0 Ret'd	3/6 6/3 6/3				
128. **Miss L.A.Davenport [2]** (USA)						

Additional bracket results:

Miss S.Williams [8] def. Miss V.Williams [5] 6/2 7/6(3)

Miss V.Williams [5] def. Miss J.Dokic 6/3 6/2 / Miss L.A.Davenport [2] 6/4 6/2

Heavy type denotes seeded players. The figure in brackets against names denotes the order in which they have been seeded.

(W) = Wild card. (Q) = Qualifier. (L) = Lucky loser.

The matches are the best of three sets

THE LADIES' DOUBLES CHAMPIONSHIP

Holders: Miss L.A.Davenport and Miss C.Morariu

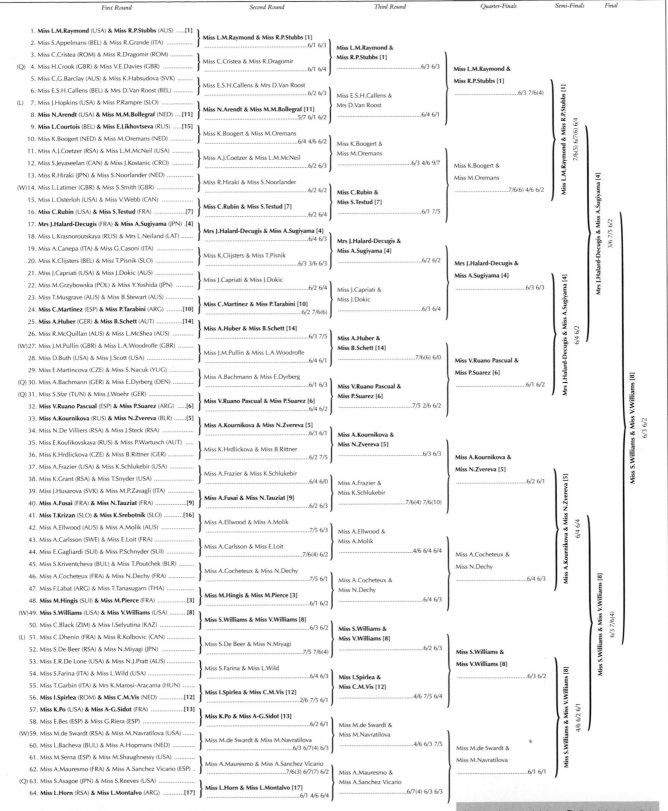

First Round · Second Round · Third Round · Quarter-Finals · Semi-Finals · Final

1. **Miss L.M.Raymond (USA) & Miss R.P.Stubbs (AUS)** .....[1]
2. Miss S.Appelmans (BEL) & Miss R.Grande (ITA) ....
3. Miss C.Cristea (ROM) & Miss R.Dragomir (ROM) ....
(Q) 4. Miss H.Crook (GBR) & Miss V.E.Davies (GBR) ....
5. Miss C.G.Barclay (AUS) & Miss K.Habsudova (SVK) ....
6. E.S.H.Callens (BEL) & Mrs D.Van Roost (BEL) ....
(L) 7. J.Hopkins (USA) & Miss P.Rampre (SLO) ....
8. **Miss N.Arendt (USA) & Miss M.M.Bollegraf (NED)** ....[11]
9. **Miss L.Courtois (BEL) & Miss E.Likhovtseva (RUS)** ....[15]
10. Miss K.Boogert (NED) & Miss M.Oremans (NED) ....
11. Miss A.J.Coetzer (RSA) & Miss L.M.McNeil (USA) ....
12. Miss S.Jeyaseelan (CAN) & Miss J.Kostanic (CRO) ....
13. Miss R.Hiraki (JPN) & Miss S.Noorlander (NED) ....
(W) 14. Miss L.Latimer (GBR) & Miss S.Smith (GBR) ....
15. Miss L.Osterloh (USA) & Miss V.Webb (CAN) ....
16. **Miss C.Rubin (USA) & Miss S.Testud (FRA)** ....[7]
17. **Mrs J.Halard-Decugis (FRA) & Miss A.Sugiyama (JPN)** .[4]
18. Miss L.Krasnoroutskaya (RUS) & Mrs L.Neiland (LAT) ...
19. Miss A.Canepa (ITA) & Miss G.Casoni (ITA) ....
20. Miss K.Clijsters (BEL) & Miss T.Pisnik (SLO) ....
21. Miss J.Capriati (USA) & Miss J.Dokic (AUS) ....
22. Miss M.Grzybowska (POL) & Miss Y.Yoshida (JPN) ....
23. Miss T.Musgrave (AUS) & Miss B.Stewart (AUS) ....
24. **Miss C.Martinez (ESP) & Miss P.Tarabini (ARG)** ....[10]
25. **Miss A.Huber (GER) & Miss B.Schett (AUT)** ....[14]
26. Miss R.McQuillan (AUS) & Miss L.McShea (AUS) ....
(W) 27. Miss J.M.Pullin (GBR) & Miss L.A.Woodroffe (GBR) ......
28. Miss D.Buth (USA) & Miss J.Scott (USA) ....
29. Miss E.Martincova (CZE) & Miss S.Nacuk (YUG) ....
(Q) 30. Miss A.Bachmann (GER) & Miss E.Dyrberg (DEN) ....
(Q) 31. Miss S.Sfar (TUN) & Miss J.Woehr (GER) ....
32. **Miss V.Ruano Pascual (ESP) & Miss P.Suarez (ARG)** ....[6]
33. **Miss A.Kournikova (RUS) & Miss N.Zvereva (BLR)** .....[5]
34. Miss N.De Villiers (RSA) & Miss J.Steck (RSA) ....
35. Miss E.Koulikovskaya (RUS) & Miss P.Wartusch (AUT) .....
36. Miss K.Hrdlickova (CZE) & Miss B.Rittner (GER) ....
37. Miss A.Frazier (USA) & Miss K.Schlukebir (USA) ....
38. Miss K.Grant (RSA) & Miss T.Snyder (USA) ....
39. Miss J.Husarova (SVK) & Miss M.P.Zavagli (ITA) ....
40. **Miss A.Fusai (FRA) & Miss N.Tauziat (FRA)** ....[9]
41. **Miss T.Krizan (SLO) & Miss K.Srebotnik (SLO)** ....[16]
42. Miss A.Ellwood (AUS) & Miss A.Molik (AUS) ....
43. Miss A.Carlsson (SWE) & Miss E.Loit (FRA) ....
44. Miss E.Gagliardi (SUI) & Miss P.Schnyder (SUI) ....
45. Miss S.Kriventcheva (BUL) & Miss T.Poutchek (BLR) ......
46. Miss A.Cocheteux (FRA) & Miss N.Dechy (FRA) ....
47. Miss F.Labat (ARG) & Miss T.Tanasugarn (THA) ....
48. **Miss M.Hingis (SUI) & Miss M.Pierce (FRA)** ....[3]
(W) 49. **Miss S.Williams (USA) & Miss V.Williams (USA)** ....[8]
50. Miss C.Black (ZIM) & Miss I.Selyutina (KAZ) ....
(L) 51. Miss C.Dhenin (FRA) & Miss R.Kolbovic (CAN) ....
52. Miss S.De Beer (RSA) & Miss N.Miyagi (JPN) ....
53. Miss E.R.De Lone (USA) & Miss N.J.Pratt (AUS) ....
54. Miss S.Farina (ITA) & Miss L.Wild (USA) ....
55. Miss T.Garbin (ITA) & Mrs K.Marosi-Aracama (HUN) ......
56. **Miss I.Spirlea (ROM) & Miss C.M.Vis (NED)** ....[12]
57. **Miss K.Po (USA) & Miss A-G.Sidot (FRA)** ....[13]
58. Miss E.Bes (ESP) & Miss G.Riera (ESP) ....
(W) 59. Miss M.de Swardt (RSA) & Miss M.Navratilova (USA) .....
60. Miss L.Bacheva (BUL) & Miss A.Hopmans (NED) ....
61. Miss M.Serna (ESP) & Miss M.Shaughnessy (USA) ....
62. Miss A.Mauresmo (FRA) & Miss A.Sanchez Vicario (ESP) .
(Q) 63. Miss S.Asagoe (JPN) & Miss S.Reeves (USA) ....
64. **Miss L.Horn (RSA) & Miss L.Montalvo (ARG)** ....[17]

Second Round

Miss L.M.Raymond & Miss R.P.Stubbs [1]
..................................6/1 6/3
Miss C.Cristea & Miss R.Dragomir
..................................6/1 6/4
Miss E.S.H.Callens & Mrs D.Van Roost
..................................6/2 6/6
Miss N.Arendt & Miss M.M.Bollegraf [11]
..................................5/7 6/1 6/2
Miss K.Boogert & Miss M.Oremans
..................................6/4 4/6 6/2
Miss A.J.Coetzer & Miss L.M.McNeil
..................................6/2 6/3
Miss R.Hiraki & Miss S.Noorlander
..................................6/2 6/2
Miss C.Rubin & Miss S.Testud [7]
..................................6/2 6/4
Mrs J.Halard-Decugis & Miss A.Sugiyama [4]
..................................6/4 6/3
Miss K.Clijsters & Miss T.Pisnik
..................................6/3 3/6 6/3
Miss J.Capriati & Miss J.Dokic
..................................6/2 6/4
Miss C.Martinez & Miss P.Tarabini [10]
..................................6/2 7/6(6)
Miss A.Huber & Miss B.Schett [14]
..................................6/3 7/5
Miss J.M.Pullin & Miss L.A.Woodroffe
..................................6/4 6/1
Miss A.Bachmann & Miss E.Dyrberg
..................................6/1 6/3
Miss V.Ruano Pascual & Miss P.Suarez [6]
..................................6/4 6/2
Miss A.Kournikova & Miss N.Zvereva [5]
..................................6/3 6/1
Miss K.Hrdlickova & Miss B.Rittner
..................................6/2 7/5
Miss A.Frazier & Miss K.Schlukebir
..................................6/4 6/0
Miss A.Fusai & Miss N.Tauziat [9]
..................................6/2 6/3
Miss A.Ellwood & Miss A.Molik
..................................7/5 6/3
Miss A.Carlsson & Miss E.Loit
..................................7/6(4) 6/2
Miss A.Cocheteux & Miss N.Dechy
..................................7/5 6/1
Miss M.Hingis & Miss M.Pierce [3]
..................................6/1 6/2
Miss S.Williams & Miss V.Williams [8]
..................................6/3 6/2
Miss S.De Beer & Miss N.Miyagi
..................................7/5 7/6(4)
Miss S.Farina & Miss L.Wild
..................................6/4 6/3
Miss I.Spirlea & Miss C.M.Vis [12]
..................................2/6 7/5 6/1
Miss K.Po & Miss A-G.Sidot [13]
..................................6/2 6/1
Miss M.de Swardt & Miss M.Navratilova
..................................6/3 6/7(4) 6/3
Miss A.Mauresmo & Miss A.Sanchez Vicario
..................................7/6(3) 6/7(7) 6/2
Miss L.Horn & Miss L.Montalvo [17]
..................................6/1 4/6 6/4

Third Round

Miss L.M.Raymond & Miss R.P.Stubbs [1]
..................................6/3 6/3
Miss E.S.H.Callens & Mrs D.Van Roost
..................................6/4 6/1
Miss K.Boogert & Miss M.Oremans
..................................6/3 4/6 9/7
Miss C.Rubin & Miss S.Testud [7]
..................................6/1 7/5
Mrs J.Halard-Decugis & Miss A.Sugiyama [4]
..................................6/2 6/2
Miss J.Capriati & Miss J.Dokic
..................................6/3 6/4
Miss A.Huber & Miss B.Schett [14]
..................................7/6(6) 6/0
Miss V.Ruano Pascual & Miss P.Suarez [6]
..................................7/5 2/6 6/2
Miss A.Kournikova & Miss N.Zvereva [5]
..................................6/3 6/3
Miss A.Frazier & Miss K.Schlukebir
..................................7/6(4) 7/6(10)
Miss A.Ellwood & Miss A.Molik
..................................4/6 6/4 6/4
Miss A.Cocheteux & Miss N.Dechy
..................................6/4 6/3
Miss S.Williams & Miss V.Williams [8]
..................................6/2 6/3
Miss I.Spirlea & Miss C.M.Vis [12]
..................................4/6 7/5 6/4
Miss M.de Swardt & Miss M.Navratilova
..................................4/6 6/3 7/5
Miss A.Mauresmo & Miss A.Sanchez Vicario
..................................6/7(4) 6/3 6/3

Quarter-Finals

Miss L.M.Raymond & Miss R.P.Stubbs [1]
..................................6/3 7/6(4)
Miss K.Boogert & Miss M.Oremans
..................................7/6(6) 4/6 6/2
Mrs J.Halard-Decugis & Miss A.Sugiyama [4]
..................................6/3 6/3
Miss V.Ruano Pascual & Miss P.Suarez [6]
..................................6/1 6/2
Miss A.Kournikova & Miss N.Zvereva [5]
..................................6/2 6/1
Miss A.Cocheteux & Miss N.Dechy
..................................6/4 6/3
Miss S.Williams & Miss V.Williams [8]
..................................6/3 6/2
Miss M.de Swardt & Miss M.Navratilova
..................................6/1 6/1

Semi-Finals

Miss L.M.Raymond & Miss R.P.Stubbs [1]
..................................7/6(5) 6/7(6) 6/4
Mrs J.Halard-Decugis & Miss A.Sugiyama [4]
..................................6/4 6/2
Miss A.Kournikova & Miss N.Zvereva [5]
..................................6/4 6/4
Miss S.Williams & Miss V.Williams [8]
..................................6/3 7/6(4)

Final

Mrs J.Halard-Decugis & Miss A.Sugiyama [4]
..................................3/6 7/5 6/2
Miss S.Williams & Miss V.Williams [8]
..................................4/6 6/2 6/1

Miss S.Williams & Miss V.Williams [8]
..................................6/3 6/2

The winners become the holders, for the year only, of the CHALLENGE CUP presented by HRH PRINCESS MARINA, DUCHESS OF KENT, the late President of The All England Lawn Tennis and Croquet Club. The winners receive silver replicas of the Challenge Cup. A silver salver is presented to each of the runners-up and a bronze medal to each defeated semi-finalist.

Heavy type denotes seeded players. The figure in brackets against names denotes the order in which they have been seeded.
(W) = Wild card. (Q) = Qualifier. (L) = Lucky loser.

The matches are the best of three sets

Holders: L.Paes and Miss L.M.Raymond

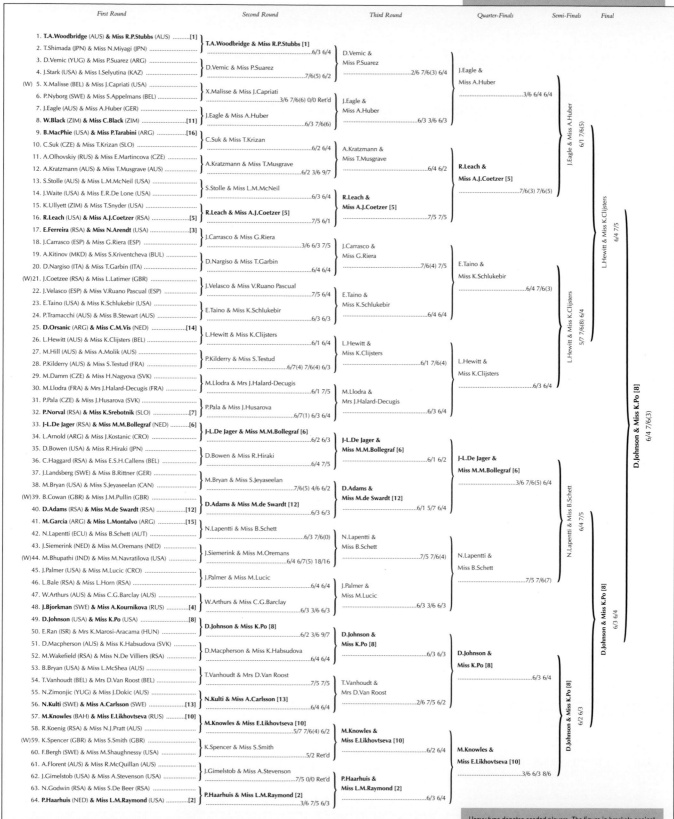

First Round	Second Round	Third Round	Quarter-Finals	Semi-Finals	Final

1. **T.A.Woodbridge** (AUS) **& Miss R.P.Stubbs** (AUS) ....[1]
2. T.Shimada (JPN) & Miss N.Miyagi (JPN) ....
3. D.Vemic (YUG) & Miss P.Suarez (ARG) ....
4. J.Stark (USA) & Miss I.Selyutina (KAZ) ....
(W) 5. X.Malisse (BEL) & Miss J.Capriati (USA) ....
6. P.Nyborg (SWE) & Miss S.Appelmans (BEL) ....
7. J.Eagle (AUS) & Miss A.Huber (GER) ....
8. **W.Black** (ZIM) **& Miss C.Black** (ZIM) ....[11]
9. **B.MacPhie** (USA) **& Miss P.Tarabini** (ARG) ....[16]
10. C.Suk (CZE) & Miss T.Krizan (SLO) ....
11. A.Olhovskiy (RUS) & Miss E.Martincova (CZE) ....
12. A.Kratzmann (AUS) & Miss T.Musgrave (AUS) ....
13. S.Stolle (AUS) & Miss L.M.McNeil (USA) ....
14. J.Waite (USA) & Miss E.R.De Lone (USA) ....
15. J.Ullyett (ZIM) & Miss T.Snyder (USA) ....
16. **R.Leach** (USA) **& Miss A.J.Coetzer** (RSA) ....[5]
17. **E.Ferreira** (RSA) **& Miss N.Arendt** (USA) ....[3]
18. J.Carrasco (ESP) & Miss G.Riera (ESP) ....
19. A.Kitinov (MKD) & Miss S.Kriventcheva (BUL) ....
20. D.Nargiso (ITA) & Miss T.Garbin (ITA) ....
(W) 21. J.Coetzee (RSA) & Miss L.Latimer (GBR) ....
22. J.Velasco (ESP) & Miss V.Ruano Pascual (ESP) ....
23. E.Taino (USA) & Miss K.Schlukebir (USA) ....
24. T.Tramacchi (AUS) & Miss B.Stewart (AUS) ....
25. **D.Orsanic** (ARG) **& Miss C.M.Vis** (NED) ....[14]
26. L.Hewitt (AUS) & Miss K.Clijsters (BEL) ....
27. M.Hill (AUS) & Miss A.Molik (AUS) ....
28. P.Kilderry (AUS) & Miss S.Testud (FRA) ....
29. M.Damm (CZE) & Miss H.Nagyova (SVK) ....
30. M.Llodra (FRA) & Mrs J.Halard-Decugis (FRA) ....
31. P.Pala (CZE) & Miss J.Husarova (SVK) ....
32. **P.Norval** (RSA) **& Miss K.Srebotnik** (SLO) ....[7]
33. **J-L.De Jager** (RSA) **& Miss M.M.Bollegraf** (NED) ....[6]
34. L.Arnold (ARG) & Miss J.Kostanic (CRO) ....
35. D.Bowen (USA) & Miss R.Hiraki (JPN) ....
36. C.Haggard (RSA) & Miss E.S.H.Callens (BEL) ....
37. J.Landsberg (SWE) & Miss B.Rittner (GER) ....
38. M.Bryan (USA) & Miss S.Jeyaseelan (CAN) ....
(W) 39. B.Cowan (GBR) & Miss J.M.Pullin (GBR) ....
40. **D.Adams** (RSA) **& Miss M.de Swardt** (RSA) ....[12]
41. **M.Garcia** (ARG) **& Miss L.Montalvo** (ARG) ....[15]
42. N.Lapentti (ECU) & Miss B.Schett (AUT) ....
43. J.Siemerink (NED) & Miss M.Oremans (NED) ....
(W) 44. M.Bhupathi (IND) & Miss M.Navratilova (USA) ....
45. J.Palmer (USA) & Miss M.Lucic (CRO) ....
46. L.Bale (RSA) & Miss L.Horn (RSA) ....
47. W.Arthurs (AUS) & Miss C.G.Barclay (AUS) ....
48. **J.Bjorkman** (SWE) **& Miss A.Kournikova** (RUS) ....[4]
49. **D.Johnson** (USA) **& Miss K.Po** (USA) ....[8]
50. E.Ran (ISR) & Mrs K.Marosi-Aracama (HUN) ....
51. D.Macpherson (AUS) & Miss K.Habsudova (SVK) ....
52. M.Wakefield (RSA) & Miss N.De Villiers (RSA) ....
53. B.Bryan (USA) & Miss L.McShea (AUS) ....
54. T.Vanhoudt (BEL) & Miss D.Van Roost (BEL) ....
55. N.Zimonjic (YUG) & Miss J.Dokic (AUS) ....
56. **N.Kulti** (SWE) **& Miss A.Carlsson** (SWE) ....[13]
57. **M.Knowles** (BAH) **& Miss E.Likhovtseva** (RUS) ....[10]
58. R.Koenig (RSA) & Miss N.J.Pratt (AUS) ....
(W) 59. K.Spencer (GBR) & Miss S.Smith (GBR) ....
60. F.Bergh (SWE) & Miss M.Shaughnessy (USA) ....
61. A.Florent (AUS) & Miss R.McQuillan (AUS) ....
62. J.Gimelstob (USA) & Miss A.Stevenson (USA) ....
63. N.Godwin (RSA) & Miss S.De Beer (RSA) ....
64. **P.Haarhuis** (NED) **& Miss L.M.Raymond** (USA) ....[2]

Second Round:

T.A.Woodbridge & Miss R.P.Stubbs [1]
D.Vemic & Miss P.Suarez ....7/6(5) 6/2
X.Malisse & Miss J.Capriati ....3/6 7/6(6) 0/0 Ret'd
J.Eagle & Miss A.Huber ....6/3 7/6(6)
C.Suk & Miss T.Krizan 6/2 6/4
A.Kratzmann & Miss T.Musgrave 6/2 3/6 9/7
S.Stolle & Miss L.M.McNeil 6/3 6/4
R.Leach & Miss A.J.Coetzer [5] 7/5 6/1
J.Carrasco & Miss G.Riera 3/6 6/3 7/5
D.Nargiso & Miss T.Garbin 6/4 6/4
J.Velasco & Miss V.Ruano Pascual 7/5 6/4
E.Taino & Miss K.Schlukebir 6/3 6/3
L.Hewitt & Miss K.Clijsters 6/1 6/4
P.Kilderry & Miss S.Testud ....6/7(4) 7/6(4) 6/3
M.Llodra & Mrs J.Halard-Decugis 6/1 7/5
P.Pala & Miss J.Husarova ....6/7(1) 6/3 6/4
J-L.De Jager & Miss M.M.Bollegraf [6] 6/2 6/3
D.Bowen & Miss R.Hiraki 6/4 7/5
M.Bryan & Miss S.Jeyaseelan ....7/6(5) 4/6 6/2
D.Adams & Miss M.de Swardt [12] 6/3 6/3
N.Lapentti & Miss B.Schett ....6/3 7/6(0)
J.Siemerink & Miss M.Oremans ....6/4 6/7(5) 18/16
J.Palmer & Miss M.Lucic 6/4 6/4
W.Arthurs & Miss C.G.Barclay 6/3 3/6 6/3
D.Johnson & Miss K.Po [8] 6/2 3/6 9/7
D.Macpherson & Miss K.Habsudova 6/4 6/4
T.Vanhoudt & Mrs D.Van Roost 7/5 7/5
N.Kulti & Miss A.Carlsson [13] 6/4 6/4
M.Knowles & Miss E.Likhovtseva [10] ....5/7 7/6(4) 6/2
K.Spencer & Miss S.Smith ....5/2 Ret'd
J.Gimelstob & Miss A.Stevenson ....7/5 0/0 Ret'd
P.Haarhuis & Miss L.M.Raymond [2] 3/6 7/5 6/3

Third Round:

D.Vemic & Miss P.Suarez ....2/6 7/6(3) 6/4
J.Eagle & Miss A.Huber 6/3 3/6 6/3
A.Kratzmann & Miss T.Musgrave 6/4 6/2
R.Leach & Miss A.J.Coetzer [5] 7/5 7/5
J.Carrasco & Miss G.Riera ....7/6(4) 7/5
E.Taino & Miss K.Schlukebir 6/4 6/4
L.Hewitt & Miss K.Clijsters ....6/1 7/6(4)
M.Llodra & Mrs J.Halard-Decugis 6/3 6/4
J-L.De Jager & Miss M.M.Bollegraf [6] 6/1 6/2
D.Adams & Miss M.de Swardt [12] 6/1 5/7 6/4
N.Lapentti & Miss B.Schett ....7/5 7/6(4)
J.Palmer & Miss M.Lucic 6/3 3/6 6/3
D.Johnson & Miss K.Po [8] 6/3 6/3
T.Vanhoudt & Mrs D.Van Roost 2/6 7/5 6/2
M.Knowles & Miss E.Likhovtseva [10] 6/2 6/4
P.Haarhuis & Miss L.M.Raymond [2] 6/3 6/4

Quarter-Finals:

J.Eagle & Miss A.Huber 3/6 6/4 6/4
R.Leach & Miss A.J.Coetzer [5] 6/4 6/2
E.Taino & Miss K.Schlukebir ....6/4 7/6(3)
L.Hewitt & Miss K.Clijsters 6/3 6/4
J-L.De Jager & Miss M.M.Bollegraf [6] ....3/6 7/6(5) 6/4
N.Lapentti & Miss B.Schett ....7/5 7/6(7)
D.Johnson & Miss K.Po [8] 6/3 6/4
M.Knowles & Miss E.Likhovtseva [10] 3/6 6/3 8/6

Semi-Finals:

J.Eagle & Miss A.Huber ....6/1 7/6(5)
L.Hewitt & Miss K.Clijsters ....5/7 7/6(8) 6/4
N.Lapentti & Miss B.Schett 6/4 7/5
D.Johnson & Miss K.Po [8] 6/2 6/3

Final:

L.Hewitt & Miss K.Clijsters 6/4 7/5
D.Johnson & Miss K.Po [8] ....6/4 7/6(3)

D.Johnson & Miss K.Po [8] ....6/4 7/6(3)

The winners become the holders, for the year only, of a Cup presented by The All England Lawn Tennis and Croquet Club. The winners receive miniature silver salvers. A silver medal is presented to each of the runners-up.

Holders: K.Flach and R.Seguso

GROUP A

	J.B. Fitzgerald (AUS) and W. Masur (AUS)	G.W. Donnelly (USA) and D. Visser (RSA)	J. Pugh (USA) and L. Shiras (USA)	K. Curren (USA) and J. Kriek (USA)	WINS	LOSSES
J.B. Fitzgerald (AUS) and W. Masur (AUS)		6/1 6/7(5) 2/6 L	6/4 6/7(1) 20/18 W	6/4 6/7(5) 8/6 W	2	1
G.W. Donnelly (USA) and D. Visser (RSA)	1/6 7/6(5) 6/2 W		6/2 6/3 W	1/6 7/6(5) 4/6 L	2	1
J. Pugh (USA) and L. Shiras (USA)	4/6 7/6(1) 18/20 L	2/6 3/6 L		2/6 2/6 L	0	3
K. Curren (USA) and J. Kriek (USA)	4/6 7/6(5) 6/8 L	6/1 6/7(5) 6/4 W	6/2 6/2 W		2	1

SEMI-FINAL: K. Curren (USA) and J. Kriek (USA)

GROUP B

	P.B. McNamara (AUS) and P.F. McNamee (AUS)	M.J. Bates (GBR) and N.A. Fulwood (GBR)	P. Slozil (CZE) and T. Smid (CZE)	S. Davis (USA) and T. Wilkison (USA)	WINS	LOSSES
P.B. McNamara (AUS) and P.F. McNamee (AUS)		4/6 2/6 L	6/4 6/3 W	4/6 4/6 L	1	2
M.J. Bates (GBR) and N.A. Fulwood (GBR)	6/4 6/2 W		6/3 6/1 W	6/2 6/2 W	3	0
P. Slozil (CZE) and T. Smid (CZE)	4/6 3/6 L	3/6 1/6 L		4/6 1/6 L	0	3
S. Davis (USA) and T. Wilkison (USA)	6/4 6/4 W	2/6 2/6 L	6/4 6/1 W		2	1

SEMI-FINAL: M.J. Bates (GBR) and N.A. Fulwood (GBR)

GROUP C

	A. Jarryd (SWE) and J. Nystrom (SWE)	M. Bahrami (IRI) and H. Leconte (FRA)	J.M. Lloyd (GBR) and C.J. Van Rensburg (RSA)	R. Krishnan (IND) and M. Pernfors (SWE)	WINS	LOSSES
A. Jarryd (SWE) and J. Nystrom (SWE)		4/6 6/3 6/2 W	6/0 6/4 W	6/4 6/1 W	3	0
M. Bahrami (IRI) and H. Leconte (FRA)	6/4 3/6 2/6 L		6/3 6/4 W	6/4 3/6 6/8 L	1	2
J.M. Lloyd (GBR) and C.J. Van Rensburg (RSA)	0/6 4/6 L	3/6 4/6 L		6/4 4/6 3/6 L	0	3
R. Krishnan (IND) and M. Pernfors (SWE)	4/6 1/6 L	4/6 6/3 8/6 W	4/6 6/4 6/3 W		2	1

SEMI-FINAL: A. Jarryd (SWE) and J. Nystrom (SWE)

GROUP D

	K. Flach (USA) and R. Seguso (USA)	B. Taroczy (HUN) and S. Zivojinovic (YUG)	S. Casal (ESP) and E. Sanchez (ESP)	B. Gilbert (USA) and J. Hlasek (SUI)	WINS	LOSSES
K. Flach (USA) and R. Seguso (USA)		6/3 6/2 W	6/4 7/6(6) W	6/3 7/6(1) W	3	0
B. Taroczy (HUN) and S. Zivojinovic (YUG)	3/6 2/6 L		5/7 3/6 L	3/6 4/6 L	0	3
S. Casal (ESP) and E. Sanchez (ESP)	4/6 6/7(6) L	7/5 6/3 W		6/1 7/5 W	2	1
B. Gilbert (USA) and J. Hlasek (SUI)	3/6 6/7(1) L	6/3 6/4 W	1/6 5/7 L		1	2

SEMI-FINAL: K. Flach (USA) and R. Seguso (USA)

FINAL: M.J. Bates (GBR) and N.A. Fulwood (GBR) 6/4 7/5 — K. Curren (USA) and J. Kriek (USA)

FINAL: K. Flach (USA) and R. Seguso (USA) 1/6 7/6(3) 9/7 — A. Jarryd (SWE) and J. Nystrom (SWE)

Divided

This event is played on a 'round robin' basis. Sixteen invited pairs are divided into four groups and each pair in each group plays the others. The pairs winning most matches are the winners of their respective groups and play semi-final and final rounds as indicated above. If matches should be equal in any group, the head-to-head result between the two pairs with the same number of wins determines the winning pair of the group.
Heavy type denotes seeded players. **The matches are the best of three sets.** The tie-break will operate at six games all in the first two sets.

The winners become the holders, for the year only, of a Cup presented by The All England Lawn Tennis and Croquet Club. The winners receive miniature silver salvers. A silver medal is presented to each of the runners-up.

Holders: B.E.Gottfried and T.R. Gullikson

First Round	Second Round	Semi-Finals	Final
1. **B.E.Gottfried** (USA) & **T.R.Gullikson** (USA) ....[1]	B.E.Gottfried & T.R.Gullikson [1]		
2. R.Drysdale (GBR) & A.Metreveli (RUS)		B.E.Gottfried & T.R.Gullikson [1]	
3. I.Nastase (ROM) & T.S.Okker (NED) 6/2 6/4	I.Nastase & T.S.Okker		
4. J.D.Newcombe (AUS) & A.D.Roche (AUS) 7/5 6/4		..............7/6(3) 6/3	
5. **R.L.Case** (AUS) & **G.Masters** (AUS) ....[4]	R.L.Case & G.Masters [4]		A.Amritraj & V.Amritraj
6. C.Dowdeswell (GBR) & C.J.Mottram (GBR) 6/3 3/6 6/3		A.Amritraj & V.Amritraj	
7. A.Amritraj (IND) & V.Amritraj (IND)	A.Amritraj & V.Amritraj		..............7/6(4) 6/3
8. K.R.Rosewall (AUS) & F.S.Stolle (AUS) 6/2 6/3		..............7/6(3) 6/3	
9. R.A.J.Hewitt (RSA) & F.D.McMillan (RSA)	R.C.Lutz & S.R.Smith		
10. R.C.Lutz (USA) & S.R.Smith (USA) 6/2 6/0		M.R.Edmondson & R.J.Frawley	P.Fleming & A.A.Mayer 6/2 6/4
11. M.R.Edmondson (AUS) & R.J.Frawley (AUS)	M.R.Edmondson & R.J.Frawley		
12. **J.Fillol** (CHI) & **R.L.Stockton** (USA) ....[3]		..............7/6(5) 7/5	
13. O.K.Davidson (AUS) & E.C.Drysdale (RSA) 6/4 6/4	P.Fleming & A.A.Mayer	P.Fleming & A.A.Mayer	
14. P.Fleming (USA) & A.A.Mayer (USA) 6/4 6/4			..............6/1 6/2
15. J.G.Alexander (AUS) & P.Dent (AUS)	J.G.Alexander & P.Dent		
16. **M.C.Riessen** (USA) & **S.E.Stewart** (USA) ....[2]	6/3 6/0	..............7/6(6) 6/3	

153

Heavy type denotes seeded players. The figure in brackets against names denotes the order in which they have been seeded.
The matches are the best of three sets. The tie-break will operate at six games all in the first two sets.

The winners become the holders, for the year only, of a Cup presented by The All England Lawn Tennis and Croquet Club. The winners receive miniature Cups. A silver medal is presented to each of the runners-up.

Holders: Mrs P.D.Smylie and Miss W.M.Turnbull

GROUP A	Miss Z.L. Garrison (USA) and Miss J.C. Russell (USA)	Mrs R. Nideffer (RSA) and Mrs Y. Vermaak (RSA)	Miss J.M. Durie (GBR) and Miss W.M. Turnbull (AUS)	Miss R. Casals (USA) and Miss B. Nagelsen (USA)	WINS	LOSSES	FINAL
Miss Z.L. Garrison (USA) and Miss J.C. Russell (USA)		6/3 3/6 6/8 L	2/6 3/6 L	W/O (6/0) (6/0) W	1	2	
Mrs R. Nideffer (RSA) and Miss Y. Vermaak (RSA)	3/6 6/3 8/6 W		6/2 6/2 W	W/O (6/0) (6/0) W	3	0	
Miss J.M. Durie (GBR) and Miss W.M. Turnbull (AUS)	6/2 6/3 W	2/6 2/6 L		6/1 6/3 W	2	1	
Miss R. Casals (USA) and Miss B. Nagelsen (USA)	W/O (0/6) (0/6) L	W/O (0/6) (0/6) L	1/6 3/6 L		0	3	

Mrs R. Nideffer (RSA) and Miss Y. Vermaak (RSA)

GROUP B	Mrs P.D. Smylie (AUS) and Miss G.R. Stevens (RSA)	Mrs G. Magers (USA) and Miss S.V. Wade (GBR)	Miss M. Jausovec (SLO) and Miss H. Mandlikova (AUS)	Miss A.E. Hobbs (GBR) and Miss B.F. Stove (NED)	WINS	LOSSES	FINAL
Mrs P.D. Smylie (AUS) and Miss G.R. Stevens (RSA)		3/6 6/3 5/7 L	6/4 3/6 4/6 L	6/4 6/7(5) 1/6 L	0	3	
Mrs G. Magers (USA) and Miss S.V. Wade (GBR)	6/3 3/6 7/5 W		6/4 6/7(4) 6/4 W	4/6 6/3 9/7 W	3	0	
Miss M. Jausovec (SLO) and Miss H. Mandlikova (AUS)	4/6 6/3 6/4 W	4/6 7/6(4) 4/6 L		4/6 6/3 6/4 W	2	1	
Miss A.E. Hobbs (GBR) and Miss B.F. Stove (NED)	4/6 7/6(5) 6/1 W	6/4 3/6 7/9 L	6/4 3/6 4/6 L		1	2	

Mrs G. Magers (USA) and Miss S.V. Wade (GBR)

Mrs R. Nideffer (RSA) and Miss Y. Vermaak (RSA) 6/4 6/2

This event is played on a 'round robin' basis. Eight invited pairs are divided into two groups and each pair in each group plays the others. The pairs winning most matches are the winners of their respective groups and play a final round as indicated above. If matches should be equal in any group, the head-to-head result between the two pairs with the same number of wins determines the winning pair of the group.

Heavy type denotes seeded players.

The matches are the best of three sets. The tie-break will operate at six games all in the first two sets.

ALPHABETICAL LIST – 35 & OVER EVENTS

GENTLEMEN

Bahrami M. (Iran)
Bates M.J. (Great Britain)
Casal S. (Spain)
Curren K. (USA)
Davis S. (USA)
Donnelly G.W. (USA)
Fitzgerald J.B. (Australia)
Flach K. (USA)

Fulwood N.A. (Great Britain)
Gilbert B. (USA)
Hlasek J. (Switzerland)
Jarryd A. (Sweden)
Kriek J. (USA)
Krishnan R. (India)
Leconte H. (France)
Lloyd J.M. (Great Britain)

Masur W. (Australia)
McNamara P.B. (Australia)
McNamee P.F. (Australia)
Nystrom J. (Sweden)
Pernfors M. (Sweden)
Pugh J. (USA)
Sanchez E. (Spain)
Seguso R. (USA)

Shiras L. (USA)
Slozil P. (Czech Republic)
Smid T. (Czech Republic)
Taroczy B. (Hungary)
Van Rensburg C.J. (South Africa)
Visser D. (South Africa)
Wilkison T. (USA)
Zivojinovic S. (Yugoslavia)

LADIES

Casals Miss R. (USA)
Durie Miss J.M. (Great Britain)
Garrison Miss Z.L. (USA)
Hobbs Miss A.E. (Great Britain)

Jausovec Miss M. (Slovenia)
Magers Mrs G. (USA)
Mandlikova Miss H. (Australia)
Nagelsen Miss B. (USA)

Nideffer Mrs R. (South Africa)
Russell Miss J.C. (USA)
Smylie Mrs P.D. (Australia)
Stevens Miss G.R. (South Africa)

Stove Miss B.F. (Netherlands)
Turnbull Miss W.M. (Australia)
Vermaak Miss Y. (South Africa)
Wade Miss S.V. (Great Britain)

ALPHABETICAL LIST – 45 & OVER EVENT

GENTLEMEN

Alexander J.G. (Australia)
Amritraj A. (India)
Amritraj V. (India)
Case R.L. (Australia)
Davidson O.K. (Australia)
Dent P. (Australia)
Dowdeswell C. (Great Britain)
Drysdale E.C. (South Africa)

Drysdale R. (Great Britain)
Edmondson M.R. (Australia)
Fillol J. (Chile)
Fleming P. (USA)
Frawley R.J. (Australia)
Gottfried B.E. (USA)
Gullikson T.R. (USA)
Hewitt R.A.J. (South Africa)

Lutz R.C. (USA)
Masters G. (Australia)
Mayer A.A. (USA)
McMillan F.D. (South Africa)
Metreveli A. (Russia)
Mottram C.J. (Great Britain)
Nastase I. (Romania)
Newcombe J.D. (Australia)

Okker T.S. (Netherlands)
Riessen M.C. (USA)
Roche A.D. (Australia)
Rosewall K.R. (Australia)
Smith S.R. (USA)
Stewart S.E. (USA)
Stockton R.L. (USA)
Stolle F.S. (Australia)

For both the Boys' Singles *and* the Boys' Doubles Championships, the winners become the holders, for the year only, of a Cup presented by The All England Lawn Tennis and Croquet Club. The winners each receive a miniature Cup and the runners-up receive mementoes.

Holder: J.Melzer

First Round	Second Round	Third Round	Quarter-Finals	Semi-Finals	Final
1. **N.Mahut [1]** ....(FRA)	N.Mahut [1] 6/1 6/1	N.Mahut [1]			
2. S.Wiespeiner ....(AUT)		.....................6/3 6/3	N.Mahut [1]		
3. J.Maigret ....(FRA)	O.Posada ....7/6(2) 6/2		.....................6/2 6/3		
4. O.Posada ....(VEN)		S.Rea		N.Mahut [1]	
(W) 5. S.Rea ....(NZL)	S.Rea 6/4 0/6 6/1	.....................6/3 6/4		.....................7/6(8) 7/5	
(W) 6. S.Mitchell ....(RSA)					
7. T.Pocock ....(GBR)	T.Pocock 6/4 4/6 7/5				
8. J.Tipsavevic [13] ....(YUG)			K.Beck		
9. **R.Valent [9]** ....(SUI)	R.Valent [9] 6/4 6/3	R.Valent [9]	.....................6/4 7/6(9)		
10. D.Coene ....(BEL)		.....................6/2 7/5			
(Q) 11. D.Munoz ....(ESP)	D.Munoz 7/5 6/1				
12. R.Bloomfield ....(GBR)		K.Beck			N.Mahut [1]
13. A.Matijevic ....(CRO)	K.Beck ....3/0 Ret'd	.....................6/4 6/3			7/6(6) 7/6(2)
14. **K.Beck** ....(SVK)					
(W) 15. J.Nelson ....(GBR)	J.Nelson ....7/5 7/6(6)				
16. **M.Abel [7]** ....(GER)					
17. **J.Johansson [3]** ....(SWE)	J.Johansson [3] ....6/4 7/6(4)				
18. A.Kennedy ....(AUS)		J.Johansson [3]			
19. S.Stadler ....(GER)	R.Lukaev 6/1 6/4	.....................7/6(5) 6/7(8) 10/8	R.Lukaev		
20. R.Lukaev ....(BUL)			.....................6/3 4/6 6/4		
21. Y.Wang ....(TPE)	Y.Wang 6/3 7/5				
(L) 22. G-C.Capuccio ....(VEN)		Y.Wang		R.Lukaev	
(W) 23. A.Banks ....(GBR)	A.Banks 2/6 7/5 12/10	.....................6/7(4) 7/6(3) 6/3		.....................6/4 3/6 6/1	
24. **B.Soares [14]** ....(BRA)					
25. **A.Falla [11]** ....(COL)	A.Falla [11] 2/6 7/5 6/1		A.Balzekas		
26. M.Emery ....(USA)		A.Balzekas	.....................6/4 6/4		
(Q) 27. A.Balzekas ....(LTU)	A.Balzekas 6/2 6/3	.....................6/3 6/4			
28. H.Sofyan ....(ARM)					N.Mahut [1]
29. L.Kubot ....(POL)	L.Kubot ....7/6(5) 2/6 8/6		L.Kubot		3/6 6/3 7/5
(Q) 30. R.Klaasen ....(RSA)		L.Kubot	.....................6/4 4/6 6/2		
31. P.Moukhometov ....(RUS)	A.Dernovskyy [8] ....7/6(5) 7/5	.....................6/3 6/4			
32. **A.Dernovskyy [8]** ....(UKR)					
33. **A.Cruciat [6]** ....(ROM)	L.Childs 6/2 6/1				
(W) 34. L.Childs ....(GBR)		L.Childs			
(Q) 35. H.Mirzadeh ....(USA)	H.Mirzadeh 7/5 6/2	.....................3/6 6/3 9/7	K.Vliegen [16]		
36. J.Medina ....(VEN)			.....................6/4 3/6 7/5		
37. I.Stelko ....(CRO)	I.Stelko 6/4 6/4				
38. Y.Abougzir ....(USA)		K.Vliegen [16]		M.Ancic [4]	
39. O.Alver ....(NOR)	K.Vliegen [16] 7/5 6/3	.....................6/4 6/4		.....................6/4 6/3	
40. **K.Vliegen [16]** ....(BEL)					
41. **M.Kokta [12]** ....(CZE)	M.Kokta [12] 7/5 6/2				
42. P-J.Nomdo ....(RSA)		M.Kokta [12]			
(L) 43. R.Russell ....(JAM)	G.Lapentti 6/1 7/5	.....................6/3 6/3	M.Ancic [4]		
(Q) 44. G.Lapentti ....(ECU)			.....................7/6(2) 4/6 9/7		
45. H.Kondo ....(JPN)	P.Marx 3/6 7/5 8/6				
46. P.Marx ....(GER)		M.Ancic [4]			M.Ancic [4]
(W) 47. S.Bohli ....(SUI)	M.Ancic [4] 6/3 6/1	.....................6/3 6/4			6/3 6/3
48. **M.Ancic [4]** ....(CRO)					
49. **A.Kracman [5]** ....(SLO)	A.Kracman [5] 6/2 6/1				
(W) 50. B.Riby ....(GBR)		A.Kracman [5]			
(Q) 51. D.Khumalo ....(ZIM)	T.Davis 4/6 6/4 6/4	.....................6/2 6/1	A.Kracman [5]		
52. T.Davis ....(USA)			.....................6/3 6/2		
53. J.Hernandez ....(MEX)	J.Hernandez 6/4 4/6 6/3				
(Q) 54. L.Radovanovich ....(NZL)		C.Villagran [15]		T.Enev [2]	
55. D.Madjarovski ....(YUG)	C.Villagran [15] ....7/6(1) 6/2	.....................6/3 6/4		.....................6/1 4/6 6/4	
56. **C.Villagran [15]** ....(ARG)					
57. **Y-H.Lu [10]** ....(TPE)	M.Smith 6/4 6/1				
(W) 58. M.Smith ....(GBR)		M.Smith			
59. A.Segodo ....(BEN)	C.Lewis 2/6 6/4 6/1	.....................6/0 6/1	T.Enev [2]		
(Q) 60. C.Lewis ....(GBR)			.....................6/2 6/2		
61. R.Karanusic ....(CRO)	R.Karanusic ....6/2 7/6(2)				
(L) 62. P.Harboe ....(CHI)		T.Enev [2]			
63. B.Groenfeld ....(GER)	T.Enev [2] 6/4 6/2	.....................6/3 6/1			
64. **T.Enev [2]** ....(BUL)					

Holders: G.Coria and D.Nalbandian

First Round	Second Round	Quarter-Finals	Semi-Finals	Final
1. **L.Childs** (GBR) **& J.Nelson** (GBR) ....[1]	L.Childs & J.Nelson [1] ....]	L.Childs & J.Nelson [1]		
2. bye &		.....................0/6 6/1 6/4	L.Childs & J.Nelson [1]	
3. T.Reid (AUS) & R.Russell (JAM)	T.Reid & R.Russell ....w/o		.....................6/3 6/4	
4. A.Dernovskyy (UKR) & P.Moukhometov (RUS)				
5. L.Radovanovich (NZL) & S.Rea (NZL)	O.Alver & M.Emery ....7/5 7/6(7)	T.Davis & A.Kennedy [5]		
6. O.Alver (NOR) & M.Emery (USA)		.....................6/4 6/4		
7. bye &	T.Davis & A.Kennedy [5]			
8. **T.Davis** (USA) **& A.Kennedy** (AUS) ....[5]				D.Coene & K.Vliegen [7]
9. **T.Enev** (BUL) **& R.Lukaev** (BUL) ....[3]	T.Enev & R.Lukaev [3]			1/6 6/4 6/3
10. bye &		T.Enev & R.Lukaev [3]		
11. R.Bloomfield (GBR) & S.Lockwood (GBR)	R.Bloomfield & S.Lockwood 6/2 2/6 7/5	.....................6/4 6/4	D.Coene & K.Vliegen [7]	
12. S.Mitchell (RSA) & P-J.Nomdo (RSA)			.....................6/3 3/6 6/3	
13. J.Medina (VEN) & R.Valent (SUI)	R.Karanusic & I.Stelko 6/3 6/4	D.Coene & K.Vliegen [7]		
14. R.Karanusic (CRO) & I.Stelko (CRO)		.....................7/6(4) 7/6(3)		
15. A.Falla (COL) & D.Munoz (ESP)	D.Coene & K.Vliegen [7] 3/6 6/3 8/6			
16. **D.Coene** (BEL) **& K.Vliegen** (BEL) ....[7]				
17. **D.Khumalo** (ZIM) **& R.Klaasen** (RSA) ....[6]	P.Harboe & G.Lapentti ....6/2 6/7(5) 6/3	S.Bohli & P.Marx		
18. P.Harboe (CHI) & G.Lapentti (ECU)		.....................7/6(8) 7/6(3)		
19. S.Bohli (SUI) & P.Marx (GER)	S.Bohli & P.Marx 7/5 6/4		K.Beck & M.Kokta [4]	
20. N.Bamford (GBR) & C.Lewis (GBR)			.....................6/2 6/3	
21. Y.Abougzir (USA) & H.Mirzadeh (USA)	T.Pocock & M.Smith 6/4 6/2	K.Beck & M.Kokta [4]		
22. T.Pocock (GBR) & M.Smith (GBR)		.....................6/0 6/3		D.Coene & K.Vliegen [7]
23. bye &	K.Beck & M.Kokta [4]			6/3 1/6 6/3
24. **K.Beck** (SVK) **& M.Kokta** (CZE) ....[4]				
25. **O.Posada** (VEN) **& C.Villagran** (ARG) ....[8]	I.Flanagan & B.Soares 6/4 6/2	L.Kubot & H.Sofyan		
26. I.Flanagan (GBR) & B.Soares (BRA)		.....................w/o	A.Banks & B.Riby	
27. L.Kubot (POL) & H.Sofyan (ARM)	L.Kubot & H.Sofyan 6/2 3/6 8/6		.....................w/o	
28. J.Hernandez (MEX) & A.Segodo (BEN)				
29. A.Banks (GBR) & B.Riby (GBR)	A.Banks & B.Riby 6/4 6/4	A.Banks & B.Riby		
30. P.Amritraj (USA) & Y.Wang (TPE)		.....................6/2 6/4		
31. bye &	H.Kondo & Y-H.Lu [2]			
32. **H.Kondo** (JPN) **& Y-H.Lu** (TPE) ....[2]				

Heavy type denotes seeded players. The figure in brackets against names denotes the order in which they have been seeded.
(W) = Wild card. (Q) = Qualifier. (L) = Lucky loser.

The matches are the best of three sets

For both the Girls' Singles *and* the Girls' Doubles Championships, the winners become the holders, for the year only, of a Cup presented by The All England Lawn Tennis and Croquet Club. The winners each receive a miniature Cup and the runners-up receive mementoes.

Holder: Miss I.Tulyaganova

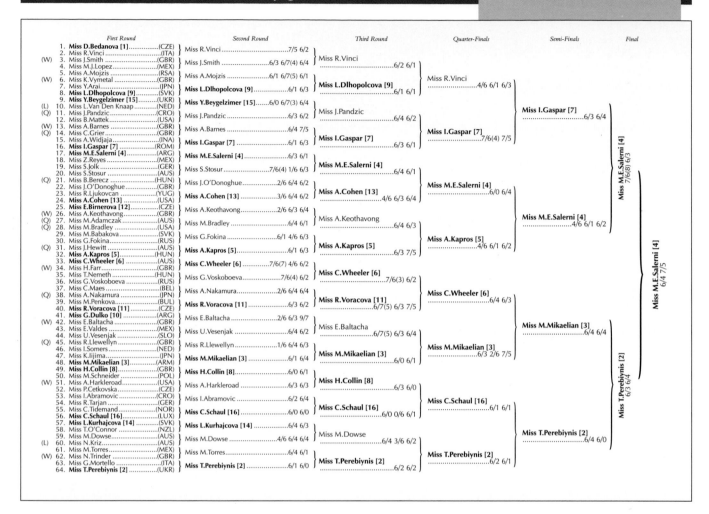

First Round
1. Miss D.Bedanova [1] (CZE)
2. Miss R.Vinci (ITA)
(W) 3. Miss J.Smith (GBR)
4. Miss M.J.Lopez (MEX)
5. Miss A.Mojzis (RSA)
(W) 6. Miss K.Vymetal (GBR)
7. Miss Y.Arai (JPN)
8. Miss L.Dlhopolcova [9] (SVK)
9. Miss Y.Beygelzimer [15] (UKR)
(L) 10. Miss L.Van Den Knaap (NED)
(Q) 11. Miss J.Pandzic (CRO)
12. Miss B.Mattek (USA)
(W) 13. Miss A.Barnes (GBR)
(Q) 14. Miss C.Grier (GBR)
15. Miss A.Widjaja (INA)
16. Miss I.Gaspar [7] (ROM)
17. Miss M.E.Salerni [4] (ARG)
18. Miss Z.Reyes (MEX)
19. Miss S.Jolk (GER)
20. Miss S.Stosur (AUS)
(Q) 21. Miss B.Berecz (HUN)
22. Miss J.O'Donoghue (GBR)
23. Miss R.Ljukovcan (YUG)
24. Miss A.Cohen [13] (USA)
25. Miss E.Birnerova [12] (CZE)
(W) 26. Miss A.Keothavong (GBR)
(Q) 27. Miss A.Adamczak (AUS)
(Q) 28. Miss M.Bradley (USA)
29. Miss M.Babakova (SVK)
30. Miss G.Fokina (RUS)
(Q) 31. Miss J.Hewitt (AUS)
32. Miss A.Kapros [5] (HUN)
33. Miss C.Wheeler [6] (AUS)
34. Miss H.Farr (GBR)
(W) 35. Miss T.Nemeth (HUN)
36. Miss G.Voskoboeva (RUS)
37. Miss C.Maes (BEL)
(Q) 38. Miss A.Nakamura (JPN)
39. Miss M.Penkova (BUL)
40. Miss R.Voracova [11] (CZE)
41. Miss G.Dulko [10] (ARG)
(W) 42. Miss E.Baltacha (GBR)
43. Miss E.Valdes (MEX)
44. Miss U.Vesenjak (SLO)
(Q) 45. Miss R.Llewellyn (GBR)
46. Miss I.Somers (NED)
47. Miss K.Iijima (JPN)
48. Miss M.Mikaelian [3] (ARM)
49. Miss H.Collin [8] (GBR)
50. Miss M.Schneider (POL)
(W) 51. Miss A.Harkleroad (USA)
52. Miss P.Cetkovska (CZE)
53. Miss I.Abramovic (CRO)
54. Miss R.Tarjan (GER)
55. Miss C.Tidemand (NOR)
56. Miss C.Schaul [16] (LUX)
57. Miss L.Kurhajcova [14] (SVK)
58. Miss T.O'Connor (NZL)
59. Miss M.Dowse (AUS)
(L) 60. Miss N.Kriz (AUS)
61. Miss M.Torres (MEX)
(W) 62. Miss N.Trinder (GBR)
63. Miss G.Mortello (ITA)
64. Miss T.Perebiynis [2] (UKR)

Second Round
Miss R.Vinci ... 7/5 6/2
Miss J.Smith ... 6/3 6/7(4) 6/4
Miss A.Mojzis ... 6/1 6/7(5) 6/1
Miss L.Dlhopolcova [9] ... 6/1 6/3
Miss Y.Beygelzimer [15] ... 6/0 6/7(3) 6/4
Miss J.Pandzic ... 6/3 6/2
Miss A.Barnes ... 6/4 7/5
Miss I.Gaspar [7] ... 6/1 6/3
Miss M.E.Salerni [4] ... 6/3 6/1
Miss S.Stosur ... 7/6(4) 1/6 6/3
Miss J.O'Donoghue ... 2/6 6/4 6/2
Miss A.Cohen [13] ... 3/6 6/4 6/2
Miss A.Keothavong ... 2/6 6/3 6/4
Miss M.Bradley
Miss G.Fokina ... 6/1 4/6 6/3
Miss A.Kapros [5] ... 6/1 6/3
Miss C.Wheeler [6] ... 7/6(7) 4/6 6/2
Miss G.Voskoboeva ... 7/6(4) 6/2
Miss A.Nakamura ... 2/6 6/4 6/4
Miss R.Voracova [11] ... 6/3 6/2
Miss E.Baltacha ... 2/6 6/3 9/7
Miss U.Vesenjak ... 6/4 6/2
Miss R.Llewellyn ... 1/6 6/4 6/3
Miss M.Mikaelian [3] ... 6/1 6/4
Miss H.Collin [8] ... 6/0 6/1
Miss A.Harkleroad ... 6/3 6/3
Miss I.Abramovic ... 6/2 6/4
Miss C.Schaul [16] ... 6/0 6/0
Miss L.Kurhajcova [14] ... 6/4 6/3
Miss M.Dowse ... 4/6 6/4 6/4
Miss M.Torres ... 6/4 6/1
Miss T.Perebiynis [2] ... 6/1 6/0

Third Round
Miss R.Vinci ... 6/2 6/1
Miss L.Dlhopolcova [9] ... 6/1 6/1
Miss J.Pandzic ... 6/4 6/2
Miss I.Gaspar [7] ... 6/3 6/1
Miss M.E.Salerni [4] ... 6/4 6/1
Miss A.Cohen [13] ... 4/6 6/3 6/4
Miss A.Keothavong ... 6/4 6/3
Miss A.Kapros [5] ... 6/3 7/5
Miss C.Wheeler [6] ... 7/6(3) 6/2
Miss R.Voracova [11] ... 6/7(5) 6/3 7/5
Miss E.Baltacha ... 6/7(5) 6/3 6/4
Miss M.Mikaelian [3] ... 6/0 6/1
Miss H.Collin [8] ... 6/3 6/0
Miss C.Schaul [16] ... 6/0 0/6 6/1
Miss M.Dowse ... 6/4 3/6 6/2
Miss T.Perebiynis [2] ... 6/2 6/2

Quarter-Finals
Miss R.Vinci ... 4/6 6/1 6/3
Miss I.Gaspar [7] ... 7/6(4) 7/5
Miss M.E.Salerni [4] ... 6/0 6/4
Miss A.Kapros [5] ... 4/6 6/1 6/2
Miss C.Wheeler [6] ... 6/4 6/3
Miss M.Mikaelian [3] ... 6/3 2/6 7/5
Miss C.Schaul [16] ... 6/1 6/1
Miss T.Perebiynis [2] ... 6/2 6/1

Semi-Finals
Miss I.Gaspar [7] ... 6/3 6/4
Miss M.E.Salerni [4] ... 4/6 6/1 6/2
Miss M.Mikaelian [3] ... 6/4 6/4
Miss T.Perebiynis [2] ... 6/4 6/0

Final
Miss M.E.Salerni [4] ... 7/6(8) 6/3
Miss T.Perebiynis [2] ... 6/3 6/4

Miss M.E.Salerni [4] ... 6/4 7/5

THE GIRLS' DOUBLES CHAMPIONSHIP

Holders: Miss D.Bedanova and Miss M.E.Salerni

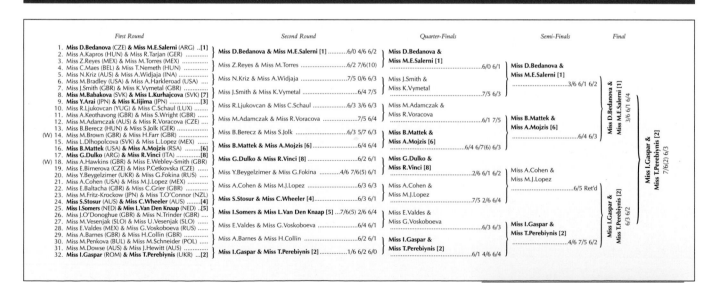

First Round
1. Miss D.Bedanova (CZE) & Miss M.E.Salerni (ARG) [1]
2. Miss A.Kapros (HUN) & Miss R.Tarjan (GER)
3. Miss Z.Reyes (MEX) & Miss M.Torres (MEX)
4. Miss C.Maes (BEL) & Miss T.Nemeth (HUN)
5. Miss N.Kriz (AUS) & Miss A.Widjaja (INA)
6. Miss M.Bradley (USA) & Miss A.Harkleroad (USA)
7. Miss J.Smith (GBR) & Miss K.Vymetal (GBR)
8. Miss M.Babakova (SVK) & Miss L.Kurhajcova (SVK) [7]
9. Miss Y.Arai (JPN) & Miss K.Iijima (JPN) [3]
10. Miss R.Ljukovcan (YUG) & Miss C.Schaul (LUX)
11. Miss A.Keothavong (GBR) & Miss S.Wright (GBR)
12. Miss M.Adamczak (AUS) & Miss R.Voracova (CZE)
13. Miss B.Berecz (HUN) & Miss S.Jolk (GER)
(W) 14. Miss M.Brown (GBR) & Miss H.Farr (GBR)
15. Miss L.Dlhopolcova (SVK) & Miss L.Lopez (MEX)
16. Miss B.Mattek (USA) & Miss A.Mojzis (RSA) [6]
17. Miss G.Dulko (ARG) & Miss R.Vinci (ITA) [8]
(W) 18. Miss A.Hawkins (GBR) & Miss E.Webley-Smith (GBR)
19. Miss E.Birnerova (CZE) & Miss P.Cetkovska (CZE)
20. Miss Y.Beygelzimer (UKR) & Miss G.Fokina (RUS)
21. Miss A.Cohen (USA) & Miss M.J.Lopez (MEX)
22. Miss E.Baltacha (GBR) & Miss C.Grier (GBR)
23. Miss M.Fritz-Krockow (JPN) & Miss T.O'Connor (NZL)
24. Miss S.Stosur (AUS) & Miss C.Wheeler (AUS) [4]
25. Miss I.Somers (NED) & Miss L.Van Den Knaap (NED) [5]
26. Miss J.O'Donoghue (GBR) & Miss N.Trinder (GBR)
27. Miss M.Vesenjak (SLO) & Miss U.Vesenjak (SLO)
28. Miss E.Valdes (MEX) & Miss G.Voskoboeva (RUS)
29. Miss A.Barnes (GBR) & Miss H.Collin (GBR)
30. Miss M.Penkova (BUL) & Miss M.Schneider (POL)
31. Miss M.Dowse (AUS) & Miss J.Hewitt (AUS)
32. Miss I.Gaspar (ROM) & Miss T.Perebiynis (UKR) [2]

Second Round
Miss D.Bedanova & Miss M.E.Salerni [1] ... 6/0 4/6 6/2
Miss Z.Reyes & Miss M.Torres ... 6/2 7/6(10)
Miss N.Kriz & Miss A.Widjaja ... 7/5 0/6 6/3
Miss J.Smith & Miss K.Vymetal ... 6/4 7/5
Miss R.Ljukovcan & Miss C.Schaul ... 6/3 3/6 6/3
Miss M.Adamczak & Miss R.Voracova ... 7/5 6/4
Miss B.Berecz & Miss S.Jolk ... 6/3 5/7 6/3
Miss B.Mattek & Miss A.Mojzis [6] ... 6/4 6/4
Miss G.Dulko & Miss R.Vinci [8] ... 6/2 6/1
Miss Y.Beygelzimer & Miss G.Fokina ... 4/6 7/6(5) 6/1
Miss A.Cohen & Miss M.J.Lopez ... 6/3 6/3
Miss S.Stosur & Miss C.Wheeler [4] ... 6/3 6/1
Miss I.Somers & Miss L.Van Den Knaap [5] ... 7/6(5) 2/6 6/4
Miss E.Valdes & Miss G.Voskoboeva ... 6/4 6/1
Miss A.Barnes & Miss H.Collin ... 6/2 6/1
Miss I.Gaspar & Miss T.Perebiynis [2] ... 1/6 6/2 6/0

Quarter-Finals
Miss D.Bedanova & Miss M.E.Salerni [1] ... 6/0 6/1
Miss J.Smith & Miss K.Vymetal ... 7/5 6/3
Miss M.Adamczak & Miss R.Voracova ... 6/1 7/5
Miss B.Mattek & Miss A.Mojzis [6] ... 6/4 6/7(6) 6/3
Miss G.Dulko & Miss R.Vinci [8] ... 2/6 6/1 6/2
Miss A.Cohen & Miss M.J.Lopez ... 7/5 2/6 6/4
Miss E.Valdes & Miss G.Voskoboeva ... 6/3 6/3
Miss I.Gaspar & Miss T.Perebiynis [2] ... 6/1 4/6 6/4

Semi-Finals
Miss D.Bedanova & Miss M.E.Salerni [1] ... 3/6 6/1 6/2
Miss B.Mattek & Miss A.Mojzis [6] ... 4/6 6/3
Miss A.Cohen & Miss M.J.Lopez ... 6/5 Ret'd
Miss I.Gaspar & Miss T.Perebiynis [2] ... 4/6 7/5 6/2

Final
Miss D.Bedanova & Miss M.E.Salerni [1] ... 3/6 6/1 6/4
Miss I.Gaspar & Miss T.Perebiynis [2] ... 6/3 6/2

Miss I.Gaspar & Miss T.Perebiynis [2] ... 7/6(2) 6/3

Heavy type denotes seeded players. The figure in brackets against names denotes the order in which they have been seeded. (W) = Wild card. (Q) = Qualifier. (L) = Lucky loser.

The matches are the best of three sets

Champions and Runners-up

Year	Champion / Runner-up
1877	S. W. Gore / *W. C. Marshall*
1878	P. F. Hadow / *S. W. Gore*
★ 1879	J. T. Hartley / *V. St. L. Goold*
1880	J. T. Hartley / *H. F. Lawford*
1881	W. Renshaw / *J. T. Hartley*
1882	W. Renshaw / *E. Renshaw*
1883	W. Renshaw / *E. Renshaw*
1884	W. Renshaw / *H. F. Lawford*
1885	W. Renshaw / *H. F. Lawford*
1886	W. Renshaw / *H. F. Lawford*
★ 1887	H. F. Lawford / *E. Renshaw*
1888	E. Renshaw / *H. F. Lawford*
1889	W. Renshaw / *E. Renshaw*
1890	W. J. Hamilton / *W. Renshaw*
★ 1891	W. Baddeley / *J. Pim*
1892	W. Baddeley / *J. Pim*
1893	J. Pim / *W. Baddeley*
1894	J. Pim / *W. Baddeley*
★ 1895	W. Baddeley / *W. V. Eaves*
1896	H. S. Mahony / *W. Baddeley*
1897	R. F. Doherty / *H. S. Mahony*
1898	R. F. Doherty / *H. L . Doherty*
1899	R. F. Doherty / *A. W. Gore*
1900	R. F. Doherty / *S. H. Smith*
1901	A. W. Gore / *R. F. Doherty*
1902	H. L. Doherty / *A. W. Gore*
1903	H. L. Doherty / *F. L. Riseley*
1904	H. L. Doherty / *F. L. Riseley*
1905 –	H. L. Doherty / *N. E. Brookes*
1906 –	H. L. Doherty / *F. L. Riseley*
★ 1907 –	N. E. Brookes / *A. W. Gore*
★ 1908 –	A. W. Gore / *H. Roper Barrett*
1909	A. W. Gore / *M. J. G. Ritchie*
1910	A. F. Wilding / *A. W. Gore*
1911	A. F. Wilding / *H. Roper Barrett*
1912	A. F. Wilding / *A. W. Gore*
1913	A. F. Wilding / *M. E. McLoughlin*
1914	N. E. Brookes / *A. F. Wilding*
1919	G. L. Patterson / *N. E. Brookes*
1920	W. T. Tilden / *G. L. Patterson*
1921	W. T. Tilden / *B. I. C. Norton*
★† 1922	G. L. Patterson / *R. Lycett*
★ 1923	W. M. Johnston / *F. T. Hunter*
★ 1924	J. Borotra / *R. Lacoste*
1925	R. Lacoste / *J. Borotra*
1926	J. Borotra / *H. Kinsey*
1927	H. Cochet / *J. Borotra*
1928	R. Lacoste / *H. Cochet*
1929	H. Cochet / *J. Borotra*
1930	W. T. Tilden / *W. Allison*
★ 1931	S. B. Wood / *F. X. Shields*
1932	H. E. Vines / *H. W. Austin*
1933	J. H. Crawford / *H. E. Vines*
1934	F. J. Perry / *J. H. Crawford*
1935	F. J. Perry / *G. von Cramm*
1936	F. J. Perry / *G. von Cramm*
★ 1937	J. D. Budge / *G. von Cramm*
1938	J. D. Budge / *H. W. Austin*
★ 1939	R. L. Riggs / *E. T. Cooke*
★ 1946	Y. Petra / *G. E. Brown*
1947	J. Kramer / *T. Brown*
★ 1948	R. Falkenburg / *J. E. Bromwich*
1949	F. R. Schroeder / *J. Drobny*
★ 1950	B. Patty / *F. A. Sedgman*
1951	R. Savitt / *K. McGregor*
1952	F. A. Sedgman / *J. Drobny*
★ 1953	V. Seixas / *K. Nielsen*
1954	J. Drobny / *K. R. Rosewall*
1955	T. Trabert / *K. Nielsen*
★ 1956	L. A. Hoad / *K. R. Rosewall*
1957	L. A. Hoad / *A. J. Cooper*
★ 1958	A. J. Cooper / *N. A. Fraser*
★ 1959	A. Olmedo / *R. Laver*
★ 1960	N. A. Fraser / *R. Laver*
1961	R. Laver / *C. R. McKinley*
1962	R. Laver / *M. F. Mulligan*
★ 1963	C. R. McKinley / *F. S. Stolle*
1964	R. Emerson / *F. S. Stolle*
1965	R. Emerson / *F. S. Stolle*
1966	M. Santana / *R. D. Ralston*
1967	J. D. Newcombe / *W. P. Bungert*
1968	R. Laver / *A. D. Roche*
1969	R. Laver / *J. D. Newcombe*
1970	J. D. Newcombe / *K. R. Rosewall*
1971	J. D. Newcombe / *S. R. Smith*
★ 1972	S. R. Smith / *I. Nastase*
★ 1973	J. Kodes / *A. Metreveli*
1974	J. S. Connors / *K. R. Rosewall*
1975	A. R. Ashe / *J. S. Connors*
1976	B. Borg / *I. Nastase*
1977	B. Borg / *J. S. Connors*
1978	B. Borg / *J. S.Connors*
1979	B. Borg / *R. Tanner*
1980	B. Borg / *J. P. McEnroe*
1981	J. P. McEnroe / *B. Borg*
1982	J. S. Connors / *J. P. McEnroe*
1983	J. P. McEnroe / *C. J. Lewis*
1984	J. P. McEnroe / *J. S. Connors*
1985	B. Becker / *K. Curren*
1986	B.Becker / *I. Lendl*
1987	P. Cash / *I. Lendl*
1988	S. Edberg / *B. Becker*
1989	B. Becker / *S. Edberg*
1990	S. Edberg / *B. Becker*
1991	M. Stich / *B. Becker*
1992	A. Agassi / *G. Ivanisevic*
1993	P. Sampras / *J. Courier*
1994	P. Sampras / *G. Ivanisevic*
1995	P. Sampras / *B. Becker*
1996	R. Krajicek / *M. Washington*
1997	P. Sampras / *C. Pioline*
1998	P. Sampras / *G. Ivanisevic*
1999	P. Sampras / *A. Agassi*

NOTE: For the years 1913, 1914 and 1919-23 inclusive the Championship Roll includes the 'World's Championship on Grass' granted to The Lawn Tennis Association by The International Lawn Tennis Federation. This title was then abolished and commencing in 1924 they became The Official Lawn Tennis Championships recognised by The International Lawn Tennis Federation. Prior to 1922 the holders in the singles events and the gentlemen's doubles did not compete in The Championships but met the winners of these events in the Challenge Rounds.
† Challenge Round abolished; holders subsequently played through. *The holder did not defend the title.

Champions and Runners-up

1884 Miss M. Watson *Miss L. Watson*	1914 Mrs. Lambert Chambers *Mrs. D. R. Larcombe*	1933 Mrs. F. S. Moody *Miss D. E. Round*	1954 Miss M. Connolly *Miss L. Brough*	1969 Mrs. P. F. Jones *Mrs. L. W. King*
1885 Miss M. Watson *Miss B. Bingley*	1919 Mlle. S. Lenglen *Mrs. Lambert Chambers*	★1934 Miss D. E. Round *Miss H. H. Jacobs*	★1955 Miss L. Brough *Mrs. J. G. Fleitz*	★1970 Mrs. B. M. Court *Mrs. L. W. King*
1886 Miss B. Bingley *Miss M. Watson*	1920 Mlle. S. Lenglen *Mrs. Lambert Chambers*	1935 Mrs. F. S. Moody *Miss H. H. Jacobs*	1956 Miss S. Fry *Miss A. Buxton*	1971 Miss E. F. Goolagong *Mrs. B. M. Court*
1887 Miss L. Dod *Miss B. Bingley*	1921 Mlle. S. Lenglen *Miss E. Ryan*	★1936 Miss H. H. Jacobs *Frau. S. Sperling*	★1957 Miss A. Gibson *Miss D. R. Hard*	1972 Mrs. L. W. King *Miss E. F. Goolagong*
1888 Miss L. Dod *Mrs. G. W. Hillyard*	†1922 Mlle. S. Lenglen *Mrs. F. Mallory*	1937 Miss D. E. Round *Miss J. Jedrzejowska*	1958 Miss A. Gibson *Miss A. Mortimer*	1973 Mrs. L. W. King *Miss C. M. Evert*
★1889 Mrs. G. W. Hillyard *Miss L. Rice*	1923 Mlle. S. Lenglen *Miss K. McKane*	★1938 Mrs. F. S. Moody *Miss H. H. Jacobs*	★1959 Miss M. E. Bueno *Miss D. R. Hard*	1974 Miss C. M. Evert *Mrs. O. Morozova*
★1890 Miss L. Rice *Miss M. Jacks*				1975 Mrs. L. W. King *Mrs. R. Cawley*
★1891 Miss L. Dod *Mrs. G. W. Hillyard*				★1976 Miss C. M. Evert *Mrs. R. Cawley*
1892 Miss L. Dod *Mrs. G. W. Hillyard*				1977 Miss S. V. Wade *Miss B. F. Stove*
1893 Miss L. Dod *Mrs. G. W. Hillyard*				1978 Miss M. Navratilova *Miss C. M. Evert*
★1894 Mrs. G. W. Hillyard *Miss E. L. Austin*				1979 Miss M. Navratilova *Mrs. J. M. Lloyd*
★1895 Miss C. Cooper *Miss H. Jackson*				1980 Mrs. R. Cawley *Mrs. J. M. Lloyd*
1896 Miss C. Cooper *Mrs. W. H. Pickering*				1981 Mrs. J. M. Lloyd *Miss H. Mandlikova*
1897 Mrs. G. W. Hillyard *Miss C. Cooper*				1982 Miss M. Navratilova *Mrs. J. M. Lloyd*
★1898 Miss C. Cooper *Miss L Martin*				1983 Miss M. Navratilova *Miss A. Jaeger*
1899 Mrs. G. W. Hillyard *Miss C. Cooper*				1984 Miss M. Navratilova *Mrs. J. M. Lloyd*
1900 Mrs. G. W. Hillyard *Miss C. Cooper*				1985 Miss M. Navratilova *Mrs. J. M. Lloyd*
1901 Mrs. A. Sterry *Mrs. G. W. Hillyard*				1986 Miss M. Navratilova *Miss H. Mandlikova*
1902 Miss M. E. Robb *Mrs. A. Sterry*				1987 Miss M. Navratilova *Miss S. Graf*
★1903 Miss D. K. Douglass *Miss E. W. Thomson*				1988 Miss S. Graf *Miss M. Navratilova*
1904 Miss D. K. Douglass *Mrs. A. Sterry*				1989 Miss S. Graf *Miss M. Navratilova*
1905 Miss M. Sutton *Miss D. K. Douglass*	1924 Miss K. McKane *Miss H. Wills*	★1939 Miss A. Marble *Miss K. E. Stammers*	1960 Miss M. E. Bueno *Miss S. Reynolds*	1990 Miss M. Navratilova *Miss Z. Garrison*
1906 Miss D. K. Douglass *Miss M. Sutton*	1925 Mlle. S. Lenglen *Miss J. Fry*	★1946 Miss P. Betz *Miss L. Brough*	★1961 Miss A. Mortimer *Miss C. C. Truman*	1991 Miss S. Graf *Miss G. Sabatini*
1907 Miss M. Sutton *Mrs. Lambert Chambers*	1926 Mrs. L. A. Godfree *Sta. L. de Alvarez*	★1947 Miss M. Osborne *Miss D. Hart*	1962 Mrs. J. R. Susman *Mrs. V. Sukova*	1992 Miss S. Graf *Miss M. Seles*
★1908 Mrs. A. Sterry *Miss A. M. Morton*	1927 Miss H. Wills *Sta. L. de Alvarez*	1948 Miss L. Brough *Miss D. Hart*	★1963 Miss M. Smith *Miss B. J. Moffitt*	1993 Miss S. Graf *Miss J. Novotna*
★1909 Miss D. P. Boothby *Miss A. M. Morton*	1928 Miss H. Wills *Sta. L. de Alvarez*	1949 Miss L. Brough *Mrs. W. du Pont*	1964 Miss M. E. Bueno *Miss M. Smith*	1994 Miss C. Martinez *Miss M. Navratilova*
1910 Mrs. Lambert Chambers *Miss D. P. Boothby*	1929 Miss H. Wills *Miss H. H. Jacobs*	1950 Miss L. Brough *Mrs. W. du Pont*	1965 Miss M. Smith *Miss M. E. Bueno*	1995 Miss S. Graf *Miss A. Sanchez Vicario*
1911 Mrs. Lambert Chambers *Miss D. P. Boothby*	1930 Mrs. F. S. Moody *Miss E. Ryan*	1951 Miss D. Hart *Miss S. Fry*	1966 Mrs. L. W. King *Miss M. E. Bueno*	1996 Miss S. Graf *Miss A. Sanchez Vicario*
★1912 Mrs. D. R. Larcombe *Mrs. A. Sterry*	★1931 Fraulein C. Aussem *Fraulein H. Krahwinkel*	1952 Miss M. Connolly *Miss L. Brough*	1967 Mrs. L. W. King *Mrs. P. F. Jones*	1997 Miss M. Hingis *Miss J. Novotna*
★1913 Mrs. Lambert Chambers *Mrs. R. J. McNair*	★1932 Mrs. F. S. Moody *Miss H. H. Jacobs*	1953 Miss M. Connolly *Miss D. Hart*	1968 Mrs. L. W. King *Miss J. A. M. Tegart*	1998 Miss J. Novotna *Miss N. Tauziat*
				1999 Miss L. A. Davenport *Miss S. Graf*

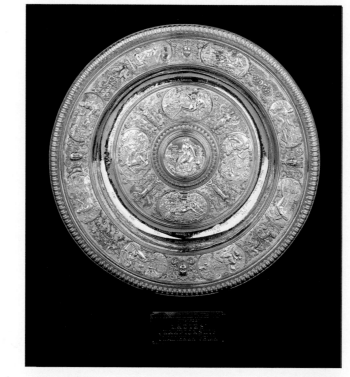

MAIDEN NAMES OF LADY CHAMPIONS
In the tables the following have been recorded in both married and single identities.

Mrs. R. Cawley .... Miss E. F. Goolagong		Mrs. F. S. Moody .... Miss H. Wills
Mrs. Lambert Chambers .... Miss D. K. Douglass	Mrs. G. W. Hillyard .... Miss B. Bingley	Mrs. O. Morozova .... Miss O. Morozova
Mrs. B. M. Court .... Miss M. Smith	Mrs. P. F. Jones .... Miss A. S. Haydon	Mrs. L. E. G. Price..................... Miss S. Reynolds
Mrs. B. C. Covell .... Miss P. L. Howkins	Mrs. L. W. King .... Miss B. J. Moffitt	Mrs. G. E. Reid .... Miss K. Melville
Mrs. D. E. Dalton .... Miss J. A. M. Tegart	Mrs. M. R. King .... Miss P. E. Mudford	Mrs. P. D. Smylie .... Miss E. M. Sayers
Mrs. W. du Pont .... Miss M. Osborne	Mrs. D. R. Larcombe .... Miss E. W. Thomson	Frau. S. Sperling .... Fraulein H. Krahwinkel
Mrs. L. A. Godfree .... Miss K. McKane	Mrs. J. M. Lloyd .... Miss C. M. Evert	Mrs. A. Sterry .... Miss C. Cooper
Mrs. H. F. Gourlay Cawley .... Miss H. F. Gourlay		Mrs. J. R. Susman .... Miss K. Hantze

GENTLEMEN'S DOUBLES

1879 L. R. Erskine and H. F. Lawford
F. Durant and G. E. Tabor
1880 W. Renshaw and E. Renshaw
O. E. Woodhouse and C. J. Cole
1881 W. Renshaw and E. Renshaw
W. J. Down and H. Vaughan
1882 J. T. Hartley and R. T. Richardson
J. G. Horn and C. B. Russell
1883 C. W. Grinstead and C. E. Welldon
C. B. Russell and R. T. Milford
1884 W. Renshaw and E. Renshaw
E. W. Lewis and E. L. Williams
1885 W. Renshaw and E. Renshaw
C. E. Farrer and A. J. Stanley
1886 W. Renshaw and E. Renshaw
C. E. Farrer and A. J. Stanley
1887 P. Bowes-Lyon and H. W. W. Wilberforce
J. H. Crispe and E. Barratt Smith
1888 W. Renshaw and E. Renshaw
P. Bowes-Lyon and H. W. W. Wilberforce
1889 W. Renshaw and E. Renshaw
E. W. Lewis and G. W. Hillyard
1890 J. Pim and F. O. Stoker
E. W. Lewis and G. W. Hillyard
1891 W. Baddeley and H. Baddeley
J. Pim and F. O. Stoker
1892 H. S. Barlow and E. W. Lewis
W. Baddeley and H. Baddeley
1893 J. Pim and F. O. Stoker
E. W. Lewis and H. S. Barlow
1894 W. Baddeley and H. Baddeley
H. S. Barlow and C. H. Martin
1895 W. Baddeley and H. Baddeley
E. W. Lewis and W. V. Eaves
1896 W. Baddeley and H. Baddeley
R. F. Doherty and H. A. Nisbet
1897 R. F. Doherty and H. L. Doherty
W. Baddeley and H. Baddeley
1898 R. F. Doherty and H. L . Doherty
H. A. Nisbet and C. Hobart
1899 R. F. Doherty and H. L. Doherty
H. A. Nisbet and C. Hobart
1900 R. F. Doherty and H. L. Doherty
H. Roper Barrett and H. A. Nisbet
1901 R. F. Doherty and H. L. Doherty
Dwight Davis and Holcombe Ward
1902 S. H. Smith and F. L. Riseley
R. F. Doherty and H. L. Doherty
1903 R. F. Doherty and H. L. Doherty
S. H. Smith and F. L. Riseley
1904 R. F. Doherty and H. L. Doherty
S. H. Smith and F. L. Riseley
1905 R. F. Doherty and H. L. Doherty
S. H. Smith and F. L. Riseley
1906 S. H. Smith and F. L. Riseley
R. F. Doherty and H. L. Doherty
1907 N. E. Brooks and A. F. Wilding
B. C. Wright and K. H. Behr
1908 A. F. Wilding and M. J. G. Ritchie
A. W. Gore and H. Roper Barrett
1909 A. W. Gore and H. Roper Barrett
S. N. Doust and H. A. Parker
1910 A. F. Wilding and M. J. G. Ritchie
A. W. Gore and H. Roper Barrett
1911 M. Decugis and A. H. Gobert
M. J. G. Ritchie and A. F. Wilding
1912 H. Roper Barrett and C. P. Dixon
M. Decugis and A. H. Gobert
1913 H. Roper Barrett and C. P. Dixon
F. W. Rahe and H. Kleinschroth
1914 N. E. Brookes and A. F. Wilding
H. Roper Barrett and C. P. Dixon
1919 R. V. Thomas and P. O'Hara-Wood
R. Lycett and R. W. Heath
1920 R. N. Williams and C. S. Garland
A. R. F. Kingscote and J. C. Parke
1921 R. Lycett and M. Woosnam
F. G. Lowe and A. H. Lowe
1922 R. Lycett and J. O. Anderson
G. L. Patterson and P. O'Hara-Wood
1923 R. Lycett and L. A. Godfree
Count de Gomar and E. Flaquer
1924 F. T. Hunter and V. Richards
R. N. Williams and W. M. Washburn
1925 J. Borotra and R. Lacoste
J. Hennessey and R. Casey
1926 H. Cochet and J. Brugnon
V. Richards and H. Kinsey
1927 F. T. Hunter and W. T. Tilden
J. Brugnon and H. Cochet
1928 H. Cochet and J. Brugnon
G. L. Patterson and J. B. Hawkes
1929 W. Allison and J. Van Ryn
J. C. Gregory and I. G. Collins
1930 W. Allison and J. Van Ryn
J. H. Doeg and G. M. Lott
1931 G. M Lott and J. Van Ryn
H. Cochet and J. Brugnon
1932 J. Borotra and J. Brugnon
G. P. Hughes and F. J. Perry
1933 J. Borotra and J. Brugnon
R. Nunoi and J. Satoh
1934 G. M. Lott and L. R. Stoefen
J. Borotra and J. Brugnon
1935 J. H. Crawford and A. K . Quist
W. Allison and J. Van Ryn
1936 G. P. Hughes and C. R. D. Tuckey
C. E. Hare and F. H. D. Wilde
1937 J. D. Budge and G. Mako
G. P. Hughes and C. R. D. Tuckey
1938 J. D. Budge and G. Mako
H. Henkel and G. von Metaxa
1939 R. L. Riggs and E. T. Cooke
C. E. Hare and F. H. D. Wilde
1946 T. Brown and J. Kramer
G. E. Brown and D. Pails
1947 R. Falkenburg and J. Kramer
A. J. Mottram and O. W. Sidwell
1948 J. E. Bromwich and F. A. Sedgman
T. Brown and G. Mulloy
1949 R. Gonzales and F. Parker
G. Mulloy and F. R. Schroeder
1950 J. E. Bromwich and A. K. Quist
G. E. Brown and O. W. Sidwell
1951 K. McGregor and F. A. Sedgman
J. Drobny and E. W. Sturgess
1952 K. McGregor and F. A. Sedgman
V. Seixas and E. W. Sturgess
1953 L. A. Hoad and K. R. Rosewall
R. N. Hartwig and M. G. Rose
1954 R. N. Hartwig and M. G. Rose
V. Seixas and T. Trabert
1955 R. N. Hartwig and L. A. Hoad
N. A. Fraser and K. R. Rosewall
1956 L. A. Hoad and K. R. Rosewall
N. Pietrangeli and O. Sirola
1957 G. Mulloy and B. Patty
N. A. Fraser and L. A. Hoad
1958 S. Davidson and U. Schmidt
A. J. Cooper and N. A. Fraser
1959 R. Emerson and N. A. Fraser
R. Laver and R. Mark
1960 R. H. Osuna and R. D. Ralston
M. G. Davies and R. K. Wilson
1961 R. Emerson and N. A. Fraser
R. A. J. Hewitt and F. S. Stolle
1962 R. A. J. Hewitt and F. S. Stolle
B. Jovanovic and N. Pilic
1963 R. H. Osuna and A. Palafox
J. C. Barclay and P. Darmon
1964 R. A. J. Hewitt and F. S. Stolle
R. Emerson and K. N. Fletcher
1965 J. D. Newcombe and A. D. Roche
K. N. Fletcher and R. A. J. Hewitt
1966 K. N. Fletcher and J. D. Newcombe
W. W. Bowrey and O. K. Davidson
1967 R. A. J. Hewitt and F. D. McMillan
R. Emerson and K. N. Fletcher
1968 J. D. Newcombe and A. D. Roche
K. R. Rosewall and F. S. Stolle
1969 J. D. Newcombe and A. D. Roche
T. S. Okker and M. C. Reissen
1970 J. D. Newcombe and A. D. Roche
K. R. Rosewall and F. S. Stolle
1971 R. S. Emerson and R. G. Laver
A. R. Ashe and R. D. Ralston
1972 R. A. J. Hewitt and F. D. McMillan
S. R. Smith and E. J. van Dillen
1973 J. S. Connors and I. Nastase
J. R. Cooper and N. A. Fraser
1974 J. D. Newcombe and A. D. Roche
R. C. Lutz and S. R. Smith
1975 V. Gerulaitis and A. Mayer
C. Dowdeswell and A. J. Stone
1976 B. E. Gottfried and R. Ramirez
R. L. Case and G. Masters
1977 R. L. Case and G. Masters
J. G. Alexander and P. C. Dent
1978 R. A. J. Hewitt and F. D. McMillan
P. Fleming and J. P. McEnroe
1979 P. Fleming and J. P . McEnroe
B. E. Gottfried and R. Ramirez
1980 P. McNamara and P. McNamee
R. C. Lutz and S. R. Smith
1981 P. Fleming and J. P. McEnroe
R. C. Lutz and S. R. Smith
1982 P. McNamara and P. McNamee
P. Fleming and J. P. McEnroe
1983 P. Fleming and J. P McEnroe
T. E. Gullikson and T. R. Gullikson
1984 P. Fleming and J. P. McEnroe
P. Cash and P. McNamee
1985 H. P. Guenthardt and B. Taroczy
P. Cash and J. B. Fitzgerald
1986 J. Nystrom and M. Wilander
G. Donnelly and P. Fleming
1987 K. Flach and R. Seguso
S. Casal and E. Sanchez
1988 K. Flach and R. Seguso
J. B. Fitzgerald and A. Jarryd
1989 J. B. Fitzgerald and A. Jarryd
R. Leach and J. Pugh
1990 R. Leach and J. Pugh
P. Aldrich and D. T. Visser
1991 J. B. Fitzgerald and A. Jarryd
J. Frana and L. Lavalle
1992 J. P. McEnroe and M. Stich
J. Grabb and R. A. Reneberg
1993 T. A. Woodbridge and M. Woodforde
G. Connell and P. Galbraith
1994 T. A. Woodbridge and M. Woodforde
G. Connell and P. Galbraith
1995 T. A. Woodbridge and M. Woodforde
R. Leach and S. Melville
1996 T. A. Woodbridge and M. Woodforde
B. Black and G. Connell
1997 T. A. Woodbridge and M. Woodforde
J. Eltingh and P. Haarhuis
1998 J. Eltingh and P. Haarhuis
T. A. Woodbridge and M. Woodforde
1999 M. Bhupathi and L. Paes
P. Haarhuis and J. Palmer

LADIES' DOUBLES

1913 Mrs. R. J. McNair and Miss D. P. Boothby
Mrs. A. Sterry and Mrs. Lambert Chambers
1914 Miss E. Ryan and Miss A. M. Morton
Mrs. D. R. Larcombe and Mrs. F. J. Hannam
1919 Mlle. S. Lenglen and Miss E. Ryan
Mrs. Lambert Chambers and Mrs. D. R. Larcombe
1920 Mlle. S. Lenglen and Miss E. Ryan
Mrs. Lambert Chambers and Mrs. D. R. Larcombe
1921 Mlle. S. Lenglen and Miss E. Ryan
Mrs. A. E. Beamish and Mrs. G. E. Peacock
1922 Mlle. S. Lenglen and Miss E. Ryan
Mrs. A. D. Stocks and Miss K. McKane
1923 Mlle. S. Lenglen and Miss E. Ryan
Miss J. Austin and Miss E. L. Colyer
1924 Mrs. H. Wightman and Miss H. Wills
Mrs. B. C. Covell and Miss K. McKane
1925 Mlle. S. Lenglen and Miss E. Ryan
Mrs. A. V. Bridge and Mrs. C. G. McIlquham
1926 Miss E. Ryan and Miss M. K. Browne
Mrs. L. A. Godfree and Miss E. L. Colyer
1927 Miss H. Wills and Miss E. Ryan
Miss E. L. Heine and Mrs. G. E. Peacock
1928 Mrs. Holcroft-Watson and Miss P. Saunders
Miss E. H. Harvey and Miss E. Bennett
1929 Mrs. Holcroft-Watson and Mrs. L. R. C. Michell
Mrs. B. C. Covell and Mrs. D. C. Shepherd-Barron
1930 Mrs. F. S. Moody and Miss E. Ryan
Miss E. Cross and Miss S. Palfrey
1931 Mrs. D. C. Shepherd-Barron and Miss P. E. Mudford
Mlle. D. Metaxa and Mlle. J. Sigart
1932 Mlle. D. Metaxa and Mlle. J. Sigart
Miss E. Ryan and Miss H. H. Jacobs
1933 Mme. R. Mathieu and Miss E. Ryan
Miss F. James and Miss A. M. Yorke
1934 Mme. R. Mathieu and Miss E. Ryan
Mrs. D. Andrus and Mme. S. Henrotin
1935 Miss F. James and Miss K. E. Stammers
Mme. R. Mathieu and Frau. S. Sperling
1936 Miss F. James and Miss K. E. Stammers
Mrs. S. P. Fabyan and Miss H. H. Jacobs
1937 Mme. R. Mathieu and Miss A. M. Yorke
Mrs. M. R. King and Mrs. J. B. Pittman
1938 Mrs. S. P. Fabyan and Miss A. Marble
Mme. R. Mathieu and Miss A. M. Yorke
1939 Mrs S. P. Fabyan and Miss A. Marble
Miss H. H. Jacobs and Miss A. M. Yorke
1946 Miss L. Brough and Miss M. Osborne
Miss P. Betz and Miss D. Hart
1947 Miss D. Hart and Mrs. P. C. Todd
Miss L. Brough and Miss M. Osborne
1948 Miss L. Brough and Mrs. W. du Pont
Miss D. Hart and Mrs. P. C. Todd
1949 Miss L. Brough and Mrs. W. du Pont
Miss G. Moran and Mrs. P. C. Todd
1950 Miss L. Brough and Mrs. W. du Pont
Miss S. Fry and Miss D. Hart
1951 Miss S. Fry and Miss D. Hart
Miss L. Brough and Mrs. W. du Pont
1952 Miss S. Fry and Miss D. Hart
Miss L. Brough and Miss M. Connolly
1953 Miss S. Fry and Miss D. Hart
Miss M. Connolly and Miss J. Sampson
1954 Miss L. Brough and Mrs. W. du Pont
Miss S. Fry and Miss D. Hart
1955 Miss A. Mortimer and Miss J. A. Shilcock
Miss S. J. Bloomer and Miss P. E. Ward
1956 Miss A. Buxton and Miss A. Gibson
Miss F. Muller and Miss D. G. Seeney
1957 Miss A. Gibson and Miss D. R. Hard
Mrs. K. Hawton and Mrs. T. D. Long
1958 Miss M. E. Bueno and Miss A. Gibson
Mrs. W. du Pont and Miss M. Varner
1959 Miss J. Arth and Miss D. R. Hard
Mrs. J. G. Fleitz and Miss C. C. Truman
1960 Miss M. E. Bueno and Miss D. R. Hard
Miss S. Reynolds and Miss R. Schuurman
1961 Miss K. Hantze and Miss B. J. Moffitt
Miss J. Lehane and Miss M. Smith
1962 Miss B. J. Moffitt and Mrs. J. R. Susman
Mrs. L. E. G. Price and Miss R. Schuurman
1963 Miss M. E. Bueno and Miss D. R. Hard
Miss R. A. Ebbern and Miss M. Smith
1964 Miss M. Smith and Miss L. R. Turner
Miss B. J. Moffitt and Mrs. J. R. Susman
1965 Miss M. E. Bueno and Miss B. J. Moffitt
Miss F. Durr and Miss J. Lieffrig
1966 Miss M. E. Bueno and Miss N. Richey
Miss M. Smith and Miss J. A. M. Tegart
1967 Miss R. Casals and Mrs. L. W. King
Miss M. E. Bueno and Miss N. Richey
1968 Miss R. Casals and Mrs. L. W. King
Miss F. Durr and Mrs. P. F. Jones
1969 Mrs. B. M. Court and Miss J. A. M. Tegart
Miss P. S. A. Hogan and Miss M. Michel
1970 Miss R. Casals and Mrs. L. W. King
Miss F. Durr and Miss S. V. Wade
1971 Miss R. Casals and Mrs. L. W. King
Mrs. B. M. Court and Miss E. F. Goolagong
1972 Mrs. L. W. King and Miss B. F. Stove
Mrs. D. E. Dalton and Miss F. Durr
1973 Miss R. Casals and Mrs. L. W. King
Miss F. Durr and Miss B. F. Stove
1974 Miss E. F. Goolagong and Miss M. Michel
Miss H. F. Gourlay and Miss K. M. Krantzcke
1975 Miss A. Kiyomura and Miss K. Sawamatsu
Miss F. Durr and Miss B. F. Stove
1976 Miss C. M. Evert and Miss M. Navratilova
Mrs. L. W. King and Miss B. F. Stove
1977 Mrs. H. F. Gourlay Cawley and Miss J. C. Russell
Miss M. Navratilova and Miss B. F . Stove
1978 Mrs. G. E. Reid and Miss. W. M. Turnbull
Miss M. Jausovec and Miss V. Ruzici
1979 Mrs. L. W. King and Miss M. Navratilova
Miss B. F. Stove and Miss W. M. Turnbull
1980 Miss K. Jordan and Miss A. E. Smith
Miss R. Casals and Miss W. M. Turnbull
1981 Miss M. Navratilova and Miss P. H. Shriver
Miss K. Jordan and Miss A. E. Smith
1982 Miss M. Navratilova and Miss P. H. Shriver
Miss K. Jordan and Miss A. E. Smith
1983 Miss M. Navratilova and Miss P. H. Shriver
Miss R. Casals and Miss W. M. Turnbull
1984 Miss M. Navratilova and Miss P. H. Shriver
Miss K. Jordan and Miss A. E. Smith
1985 Miss K. Jordan and Mrs. P. D. Smylie
Miss M. Navratilova and Miss P. H. Shriver
1986 Miss M. Navratilova and Miss P. H. Shriver
Miss H. Mandlikova and Miss W. M. Turnbull
1987 Miss C. Kohde-Kilsch and Miss H. Sukova
Miss B. Nagelsen and Mrs. P. D. Smylie
1988 Miss S. Graf and Miss G. Sabatini
Miss L. Savchenko and Miss N. Zvereva
1989 Miss J. Novotna and Miss H. Sukova
Miss L. Savchenko and Miss N. Zvereva
1990 Miss J. Novotna and Miss H. Sukova
Miss K. Jordan and Mrs. P. D. Smylie
1991 Miss L. Savchenko and Miss N. Zvereva
Miss G. Fernandez and Miss J. Novotna
1992 Miss G. Fernandez and Miss N. Zvereva
Miss J. Novotna and Mrs. L. Savchenko-Neiland
1993 Miss G. Fernandez and Miss N. Zvereva
Mrs. L. Neiland and Miss J. Novotna
1994 Miss G. Fernandez and Miss N. Zvereva
Miss J. Novotna and Miss A. Sanchez Vicario
1995 Miss J. Novotna and Miss A. Sanchez Vicario
Miss G. Fernandez and Miss N. Zvereva
1996 Miss M. Hingis and Miss H. Sukova
Miss M. J. McGrath and Mrs. L. Neiland
1997 Miss G. Fernandez and Miss N. Zvereva
Miss N. J. Arendt and Miss M. M. Bollegraf
1998 Miss M. Hingis and Miss J. Novotna
Miss L. A. Davenport and Miss N. Zvereva
1999 Miss L. A. Davenport and Miss C. Morariu
Miss M. de Swardt and Miss E. Tatarkova

MIXED DOUBLES

1913	Hope Crisp and Mrs. C. O. Tuckey *J. C. Parke and Mrs. D. R. Larcombe*	1949	E. W. Sturgess and Mrs. S. P. Summers *J. E. Bromwich and Miss L. Brough*	1975	M. C. Riessen and Mrs. B. M. Court *A. J. Stone and Miss B. F. Stove*
1914	J. C. Parke and Mrs. D.R. Larcombe *A. F. Wilding and Mlle. M. Broquedis*	1950	E. W. Sturgess and Miss L. Brough *G. E. Brown and Mrs. P. C. Todd*	1976	A. D. Roche and Miss F. Durr *R. L. Stockton and Miss R. Casals*
1919	R. Lycett and Miss E. Ryan *A. D. Prebble and Mrs. Lambert Chambers*	1951	F. A. Sedgman and Miss D. Hart *M. G. Rose and Mrs. N. M. Bolton*	1977	R. A. J. Hewitt and Miss G. R. Stevens *F. D. McMillan and Miss B. F. Stove*
1920	G. L. Patterson and Mlle. S. Lenglen *R. Lycett and Miss E. Ryan*	1952	F. A. Sedgman and Miss D. Hart *E. Morea and Mrs. T. D. Long*	1978	F. D. McMillan and Miss B. F. Stove *R. O. Ruffels and Mrs. L. W. King*
1921	R. Lycett and Miss E. Ryan *M. Woosnam and Miss P. L. Howkins*	1953	V. Seixas and Miss D. Hart *E. Morea and Miss S. Fry*	1979	R. A. J. Hewitt and Miss G. R. Stevens *F. D. McMillan and Miss B. F. Stove*
1922	P. O'Hara-Wood and Mlle. S. Lenglen *R. Lycett and Miss E. Ryan*	1954	V. Seixas and Miss D. Hart *K. R. Rosewall and Mrs. W. du Pont*	1980	J. R. Austin and Miss T. Austin *M. R. Edmondson and Miss D. L. Fromholtz*
1923	R. Lycett and Miss E. Ryan *L. S. Deane and Mrs. D. C. Shepherd-Barron*	1955	V. Seixas and Miss D. Hart *E. Morea and Miss L. Brough*	1981	F. D. McMillan and Miss B. F. Stove *J. R. Austin and Miss T. Austin*
1924	J. B. Gilbert and Miss K. McKane *L. A. Godfree and Mrs. D. C. Shepherd-Barron*	1956	V. Seixas and Miss S. Fry *G. Mulloy and Miss A. Gibson*	1982	K. Curren and Miss A. E. Smith *J. M. Lloyd and Miss W. M. Turnbull*
1925	J. Borotra and Mlle. S. Lenglen *H. L. de Morpurgo and Miss E. Ryan*	1957	M. G. Rose and Miss D. R. Hard *N. A. Fraser and Miss A. Gibson*	1983	J. M. Lloyd and Miss W. M. Turnbull *S. Denton and Mrs. L. W. King*
1926	L. A. Godfree and Mrs. L. A. Godfree *H. Kinsey and Miss M. K. Browne*	1958	R. N. Howe and Miss L. Coghlan *K. Nielsen and Miss A. Gibson*	1984	J. M. Lloyd and Miss W. M. Turnbull *S. Denton and Miss K. Jordan*
1927	F. T. Hunter and Miss E. Ryan *L. A. Godfree and Mrs. L. A. Godfree*	1959	R. Laver and Miss D. R. Hard *N. A. Fraser and Miss M. E. Bueno*	1985	P. McNamee and Miss M. Navratilova *J. B. Fitzgerald and Mrs. P. D. Smylie*
1928	P. D. B. Spence and Miss E. Ryan *J. Crawford and Miss D. Akhurst*	1960	R. Laver and Miss D. R. Hard *R. N. Howe and Miss M. E. Bueno*	1986	K. Flach and Miss K. Jordan *H. P. Guenthardt and Miss M. Navratilova*
1929	F. T. Hunter and Miss H. Wills *I. G. Collins and Miss J. Fry*	1961	F. S. Stolle and Miss L. R. Turner *R. N. Howe and Miss E. Buding*	1987	M. J. Bates and Miss J. M. Durie *D. Cahill and Miss N. Provis*
1930	J. H. Crawford and Miss E. Ryan *D. Prenn and Fraulein H. Krahwinkel*	1962	N. A. Fraser and Mrs. W. du Pont *R. D. Ralston and Miss A. S. Haydon*	1988	S. E. Stewart and Miss Z. L. Garrison *K. Jones and Mrs. S. W. Magers*
1931	G. M. Lott and Mrs L. A. Harper *I. G. Collins and Miss J. C. Ridley*	1963	K. N. Fletcher and Miss M. Smith *R. A. J. Hewitt and Miss D. R. Hard*	1989	J. Pugh and Miss J. Novotna *M. Kratzmann and Miss J. M. Byrne*
1932	E. Maier and Miss E. Ryan *H. C. Hopman and Mlle. J. Sigart*	1964	F. S. Stolle and Miss L. R. Turner *K. N. Fletcher and Miss M. Smith*	1990	R. Leach and Miss Z. L. Garrison *J. B. Fitzgerald and Mrs P. D. Smylie*
1933	G. von Cramm and Fraulein H. Krahwinkel *N. G. Farquharson and Miss M. Heeley*	1965	K. N. Fletcher and Miss M. Smith *A. D. Roche and Miss J. A. M. Tegart*	1991	J. B. Fitzgerald and Mrs. P. D. Smylie *J. Pugh and Miss N. Zvereva*
1934	R. Miki and Miss D. E. Round *H. W. Austin and Mrs D. C. Shepherd-Barron*	1966	K. N. Fletcher and Miss M. Smith *R. D. Ralston amd Mrs. L. W. King*	1992	C. Suk and Mrs L. Savchenko-Neiland *J. Eltingh and Miss M. Oremans*
1935	F. J. Perry and Miss D. E. Round *H. C. Hopman and Mrs. H. C. Hopman*	1967	O. K. Davidson and Mrs. L. W. King *K. N. Fletcher and Miss M. E. Bueno*	1993	M. Woodforde and Miss M. Navratilova *T. Nijssen and Miss M. M. Bollegraf*
1936	F. J. Perry and Miss D. E. Round *J. D. Budge and Mrs. S. P. Fabyan*	1968	K. N. Fletcher and Mrs. B. M. Court *A. Metreveli and Miss O. Morozova*	1994	T. A. Woodbridge and Miss H. Sukova *T. J. Middleton and Miss L. M. McNeil*
1937	J. D. Budge and Miss A. Marble *Y. Petra and Mme. R. Mathieu*	1969	F. S. Stolle and Mrs. P. F. Jones *A. D. Roche and Miss J. A. M. Tegart*	1995	J. Stark and Miss M. Navratilova *C. Suk and Miss G. Fernandez*
1938	J. D. Budge and Miss A. Marble *H. Henkel and Mrs. S. P. Fabyan*	1970	I. Nastase and Miss R. Casals *A. Metreveli and Miss O. Morozova*	1996	C. Suk and Miss H. Sukova *M. Woodforde and Mrs. L. Neiland*
1939	R. L. Riggs and Miss A. Marble *F. H. D. Wilde and Miss N. B. Brown*	1971	O. K. Davidson and Mrs. L. W. King *M. C. Riessen and Mrs. B. M. Court*	1997	C. Suk and Miss H. Sukova *A. Olhovskiy and Mrs. L. Neiland*
1946	T. Brown and Miss L. Brough *G. E. Brown and Miss D. Bundy*	1972	I. Nastase and Miss R. Casals *K. G. Warwick and Miss E. F. Goolagong*	1998	M. Mirnyi and Miss S. Williams *M. Bhupathi and Miss M. Lucic*
1947	J. E. Bromwich and Miss L. Brough *C. F. Long and Mrs. N. M. Bolton*	1973	O. K. Davidson and Mrs. L. W. King *R. Ramirez and Miss J. S. Newberry*	1999	L. Paes and Miss L.M. Raymond *J. Bjorkman and Miss A. Kournikova*
1948	J. E. Bromwich and Miss L. Brough *F.A. Sedgman and Miss D. Hart*	1974	O. K. Davidson and Mrs. L. W. King *M. J. Farrell and Miss L. J. Charles*		

THE JUNIOR CHAMPIONSHIP ROLL

BOYS' SINGLES

1947	K. Nielsen (Denmark)	1961	C. E. Graebner (U.S.A.)	1975	C. J. Lewis (N.Z.)	1989	N. Kulti (Sweden)
1948	S. Stockenberg (Sweden)	1962	S. Matthews (G.B.)	1976	H. Guenthardt (Switzerland)	1990	L. Paes (India)
1949	S. Stockenberg (Sweden)	1963	N. Kalogeropoulos (Greece)	1977	V. A. Winitsky (U.S.A.)	1991	T. Enquist (Sweden)
1950	J. A. T. Horn (G.B.)	1964	I. El Shafei (U.A.R.)	1978	I. Lendl (Czechoslovakia)	1992	D. Skoch (Czechoslovakia)
1951	J. Kupferburger (S.A.)	1965	V. Korotkov (U.S.S.R.)	1979	R. Krishnan (India)	1993	R. Sabau (Romania)
1952	R. K. Wilson (G.B.)	1966	V. Korotkov (U.S.S.R.)	1980	T. Tulasne (France)	1994	S. Humphries (U.S.A.)
1953	W. A. Knight (G.B.)	1967	M. Orantes (Spain)	1981	M. W. Anger (U.S.A.)	1995	O. Mutis (France)
1954	R. Krishnan (India)	1968	J. G. Alexander (Australia)	1982	P. Cash (Australia)	1996	V. Voltchkov (Belarus)
1955	M. P. Hann (G.B.)	1969	B. Bertram (S.A.)	1983	S. Edberg (Sweden)	1997	W. Whitehouse (South Africa)
1956	R. Holmberg (U.S.A.)	1970	B. Bertram (S.A.)	1984	M. Kratzmann (Australia)	1998	R. Federer (Switzerland)
1957	J. I. Tattersall (G.B.)	1971	R. Kreiss (U.S.A.)	1985	L. Lavalle (Mexico)	1999	J. Melzer (Austria)
1958	E. Buchholz (U.S.A.)	1972	B. Borg (Sweden)	1986	E. Velez (Mexico)		
1959	T. Lejus (U.S.S.R.)	1973	W. Martin (U.S.A.)	1987	D. Nargiso (Italy)		
1960	A. R. Mandelstam (S.A.)	1974	W. Martin (U.S.A.)	1988	N. Pereira (Venezuela)		

BOYS' DOUBLES

1982	P. Cash and J. Frawley	1988	J. Stoltenberg and T. Woodbridge	1994	B. Ellwood and M. Philippoussis
1983	M. Kratzmann and S. Youl	1989	J. Palmer and J. Stark	1995	M. Lee and J.M. Trotman
1984	R. Brown and R. Weiss	1990	S. Lareau and S. Leblanc	1996	D. Bracciali and J. Robichaud
1985	A. Moreno and J. Yzaga	1991	K. Alami and G. Rusedski	1997	L. Horna and N. Massu
1986	T. Carbonell and P. Korda	1992	S. Baldas and S. Draper	1998	R. Federer and O. Rochus
1987	J. Stoltenberg and T. Woodbridge	1993	S. Downs and J. Greenhalgh	1999	G. Coria and D. Nalbandian

GIRLS' SINGLES

1947	Miss B. Domken (Belgium)	1961	Miss G. Baksheeva (U.S.S.R.)	1975	Miss N.Y. Chmyreva (U.S.S.R.)	1989	Miss A. Strnadova (Czechoslavakia)
1948	Miss O. Miskova (Czechoslovakia)	1962	Miss G. Baksheeva (U.S.S.R.)	1976	Miss N.Y. Chmyreva (U.S.S.R.)	1990	Miss A. Strnadova (Czechoslavakia)
1949	Miss C. Mercelis (Belgium)	1963	Miss D. M. Salfati (France)	1977	Miss L. Antoniplis (U.S.A.)	1991	Miss B. Rittner (Germany)
1950	Miss L. Cornell (G.B.)	1964	Miss P. Bartkowicz (U.S.A.)	1978	Miss T. Austin (U.S.A.)	1992	Miss C. Rubin (U.S.A.)
1951	Miss L. Cornell (G.B.)	1965	Miss O. Morozova (U.S.S.R.)	1979	Miss M. L. Piatek (U.S.A.)	1993	Miss N. Feber (Belgium)
1952	Miss ten Bosch (Netherlands)	1966	Miss B. Lindstrom (Finland)	1980	Miss D. Freeman (Australia)	1994	Miss M. Hingis (Switzerland)
1953	Miss D. Kilian (S.A.)	1967	Miss J. Salome (Netherlands)	1981	Miss Z. Garrison (U.S.A.)	1995	Miss A. Olsza (Poland)
1954	Miss V. A. Pitt (G.B.)	1968	Miss K. Pigeon (U.S.A.)	1982	Miss C. Tanvier (France)	1996	Miss A. Mauresmo (France)
1955	Miss S. M. Armstrong (G.B.)	1969	Miss K. Sawamatsu (Japan)	1983	Miss P. Paradis (France)	1997	Miss C. Black (Zimbabwe)
1956	Miss A. S. Haydon (G.B.)	1970	Miss S. Walsh (U.S.A.)	1984	Miss A. N. Croft (G.B.)	1998	Miss K. Srebotnik (Slovenia)
1957	Miss M. Arnold (U.S.A.)	1971	Miss M. Kroschina (U.S.S.R.)	1985	Miss A. Holikova (Czechoslovakia)	1999	Miss I. Tulyagnova (Uzbekhistan)
1958	Miss S. M. Moore (U.S.A.)	1972	Miss I. Kloss (S.A.)	1986	Miss N. Zvereva (U.S.S.R.)		
1959	Miss J. Cross (S.A.)	1973	Miss A. Kiyomura (U.S.A.)	1987	Miss N. Zvereva (U.S.S.R.)		
1960	Miss K. Hantze (U.S.A.)	1974	Miss M. Jausovec (Yugoslavia)	1988	Miss B. Schultz (Netherlands)		

GIRLS' DOUBLES

1982	Miss B. Herr and Miss P. Barg	1988	Miss J. A. Faull and Miss R. McQuillan	1994	Miss E. De Villiers and Miss E. E. Jelfs
1983	Miss P. Fendick and Miss P. Hy	1989	Miss J. Capriati and Miss M. McGrath	1995	Miss C. Black and Miss A. Olsza
1984	Miss C. Kuhlman and Miss S. Rehe	1990	Miss K. Habsudova and Miss A. Strnadova	1996	Miss O. Barabanschikova and Miss A. Mauresmo
1985	Miss L. Field and Miss J. Thompson	1991	Miss C. Barclay and Miss L. Zaltz	1997	Miss C. Black and Miss I. Selyutina
1986	Miss M. Jaggard and Miss L. O'Neill	1992	Miss M. Avotins and Miss L. McShea	1998	Miss E. Dyrberg and Miss J. Kostanic
1987	Miss N. Medvedeva and Miss N. Zvereva	1993	Miss L. Courtois and Miss N. Feber	1999	Miss D. Bedanova and Miss M.E. Salerni